STUCK IN HALFTIME

REINVESTING YOUR ONE AND ONLY LIFE

Resources by Bob Buford

Halftime
Halftime Zondervan*Groupware™*
Game Plan
Halftime/Game Plan audio
Stuck in Halftime
Stuck in Halftime audio

STUCK IN HALFTIME

REINVESTING YOUR ONE AND ONLY LIFE

BOB BUFORD

AUTHOR OF *Halftime*

FOREWORD BY **PETER DRUCKER**

GRAND RAPIDS, MICHIGAN 49530 USA

Stuck in Halftime
Copyright © 2001 by Leadership Network, Inc.

Requests for information should be addressed to:

ZONDERVAN
Grand Rapids, Michigan 49530

Library of Congress Cataloging-in-Publication Data
Buford, Bob.
    Stuck in halftime : reinventing your one and only life / Bob Buford.
      p. cm.
    ISBN 0-310-23583-9
    1. Middle aged persons — Religious life. 2. Middle age — Psychological aspects 3.
Self-realization — Religious aspects — Christianity. I. Title.
BV4579.5 B845 2001
248.8'4 — dc21
                                               00-068044
                                                CIP

This edition printed on acid-free paper.

All Scripture quotations, unless otherwise indicated, are taken from the *Holy Bible: New International Version*®. NIV®. Copyright © 1973, 1978, 1984 by International Bible Society. Used by permission of Zondervan Publishing House. All rights reserved.

Interior design by Todd Sprague

Printed in the United States of America

---

01 02 03 04 05 06 07 /❖ DC/ 10 9 8 7 6 5 4 3 2 1

A pier is nothing other than a frustrated bridge. It is connected to one shore only and does not have another shore to attach itself to.

Shimon Peres

CONTENTS

THE WORLD IS FULL OF OPTIONS

In a few hundred years, when the history of our time is written from a long-term perspective, I think it very probable that the most important event those historians will remember is not technology, not the Internet, not e-commerce—but the unprecedented change in the human condition. For the first time—and I mean that literally—substantial and rapidly growing numbers of people have choices. For the first time, people have had to *manage themselves.*

And we are totally unprepared for it.

Up until around 1900, even in the most highly developed countries, the overwhelming majority of people simply followed in their father's footsteps—if they were lucky. If your father was a peasant farmer, you were a peasant farmer. If he was a craftsman, you were a craftsman. There was no such thing as upward mobility.

Now, suddenly, a large number of people choose what they want to be. And what's more, they have more than one career. The average working life span is now close to sixty years. In 1900, it was twenty.

In a short time, we will no longer believe that retirement means the end of working life. Retirement may even come much earlier than ever, but working life will continue if only out of economic necessity. For many, however, working well beyond retirement will be a choice based on preference. They will either tire of luxury or desire to use their knowledge and experience to contribute to society.

Even during their now traditional thirty- to forty-year working lives, most people have options that never existed for their parents, and they exercise those options several times. When I talk to the people in my executive management program (successful people who are forty-five years old on average, sixty percent of whom are in the business sector, forty percent in nonbusiness), everyone says, "I do not expect to end my career where I am working now."

To take advantage of this unprecedented age of options, we need to learn who we are. We don't know. When I ask my students, "Do you know what you're good at?" almost no one knows. "Do you know what you need to learn to get the full benefit of your strengths?" Not one of them has even asked that question.

Few people know where they belong, what kind of temperament they have, or what kind of person they are. "Do I work well with people or am I a loner?" "What are my values?" "What am I committed to?" "Where do I belong?" "What is my contribution?"

Many people intuitively know the answers to these questions, but because they do not work through them systematically, they often sell themselves short. So we find ourselves in an unprecedented place: The most educated people in history, with a world full of options for meaningful work, and yet unsure of just where we belong.

Those who want to live a fulfilling life—who want to feel as if there is some purpose in their being on this earth—will have to learn to manage themselves. They will have to accept the fact that it is their own responsibility to find meaningful work that builds on their strengths and values.

As this happens, I believe more and more people will look to the social sector—volunteer organizations like the church, education, community services, and so on—for either a new career or one that parallels a current position. This is the one place where the knowledgeable worker in an organization can actually discover who he or she is and can learn to manage him or herself.

Bob Buford has done a great service in his first book, *Halftime,* by showing people how to explore this wonderful world of options. In this book he offers encouragement and motivation for those who have begun to seek their "Second Half career" but are not quite there...yet.

Do You Feel It?

Lots of people are going to waste the Second Half of their lives, but there are those who are receptive.
Peter Drucker
June 16, 2000

Like many businessmen, I did not want to give up my position, my status, and the prestige that went along with being the CEO.
A Chief Executive Officer

Men lust, but they know not what for. They fight and compete, but they forget the prize; they spread seed, but spurn the seasons of growth; they chase power and glory, but miss the meaning of life.
George Gilder

Uh-oh! Something is happening...and just when you were beginning to feel you had it made...that life's big issues were put to bed...that the kids were headed for college...that your work had settled into a comfortable routine...now that most of what you have worked for has paid off, why do you feel as if you're still missing something?

It usually begins toward the end of your third decade. Or shortly after the big "four-oh" bash. It is not a bad feeling—simply the sense that something not entirely pleasant is just around the corner. Sometimes it comes in the form of questions about your contribution. Is what I'm doing important? Does it matter to anyone but me? Sometimes it comes in the form of uncertainty about your finances. Do I have enough?

Enough for what? You certainly have enough for right now. If you are like most people in your generation, you are more comfortable than your parents were as they approached midlife. You probably own more of your home than the bank does. You earn a decent salary and enjoy remarkable benefits. Although you work hard, you also have more free time than your counterparts from previous generations. And to keep you from boredom during that free time, you have all the toys you need. Probably more.

But the future concerns you. Do you have enough in the college fund for your kids? Enough for weddings and maybe a nice place at the lake? Enough for...but you can't really bring yourself to say it. You dismiss the thought that someday you will leave what you are doing in your career and...well, what?

Retirement is not in your vocabulary.

Then it returns. You are enjoying the fruits of your labor. Money is not as much of a worry as it once was. Your kids have the things you never had when you were their age. Except for one thing—they don't have as much of you as you had of your mom or dad. You got where you are by working hard, going the extra mile. Staying there demands the same level of dedication. You begin to wonder. Do you really want to stay there? Is the payoff worth the effort?

You look around and see something no other generation of Americans has seen: men and women in the prime of life walking away from their work. Cashing out and following their dreams. It looks good, and you begin looking more carefully at your own assets. Between the success of your mutual fund and the generous gift from the estate of your wife's parents, you just might be able to do it. Quit your job, maybe do a little something on the side, but finally have the freedom to do the things you never had time for during the First Half of your working life:

> Make every one of your daughter's soccer games
>
> Take that trip to Hawaii, and many more trips with your spouse
>
> Spend more time on your boat
>
> Finally read the books that you *want* to read, not the periodicals you have to read in order to stay current at work
>
> Work on your spiritual side. Take a retreat. Develop a consistent pattern of meditation and study
>
> Give a little more of yourself to that charity that gets a check from you once a year

You begin to imagine how your life would look once you cut the ties with your job. You mentally play out your daily schedule. No more rushing off with a cup of coffee for the daily commute, but a more relaxed entry into the day. Long weekend camping trips with your kids. Midday "dates" with your spouse. Maybe you'll even have time to do the exercising your doctor keeps nagging you to do.

It begins to look good. Real good. But you don't know what to call it. It's not retirement. You saw what happened to your dad when he retired. After giving forty years to the same company, he got his gold watch and a generous pension, went south to live with other retirees, and died within three years. Retirement is for old people, and you're not old. You are barely fifty. You feel great. And you've paid attention to the demographics. You really do have at least twenty-five years of active, healthy, and dynamic living ahead of you. You don't want to spend it doing what you've been doing for the past thirty years, but you don't want to spend it in a rocking chair either.

You know what you feel, but you don't exactly know what you want.

What you are feeling is normal; what you want is reachable. You are part of the first generation in America who can even think about it. What you want is to see the next twenty-five to thirty years of your life as the best years of your life. You want to exit the rat race, but you don't want to quit *doing*. You think you'd like to quit your job, but then again you need some source of income. More important, you need something that makes you want to get up in the morning. And you have this nagging sense that instead of working just for the money, you'd like to do something that counts. Something that matters. Something that in and of itself energizes you—plays to the real you inside that has been hidden by the demands of career and family.

You are in Halftime. The awkward, disconcerting place between a hard-charging and successful First Half of your career and the unknown: the next twenty to thirty years that will make up the Second Half of your life. Amidst the many uncertainties sits a clear and unmistakable fact: You do not want to—you may not even be able to—continue doing what you do with the same level of intensity and passion. Something has to change, and you would prefer to have a hand in just what that change looks like.

Based on my own experiences and my observations of others who have exchanged the language of crisis for one of opportunity when it comes to midlife, I wrote a book called *Halftime.* I intended to show others in our generation how to move from success to significance, for that is what I believe is the unspoken desire for most of us. We have enjoyed about as much success as we want or are capable of achieving. We have seen it for what it is—a pleasant outcome and reward for hard work and talent, but only a temporary and constantly moving target. If possible, we would like to aim for something more in line with our deepest desires, more long lasting. Something that *matters.*

We are beginning to think about legacy, not in a morbid, end-of-life way, but in terms of being able to have some control over what that legacy will be.

More than 150,000 copies of *Halftime* have been sold, and it is still going strong. I have talked to hundreds of people since it was released five years ago, and it is clear that the book hit a nerve. It validated the emotions so many people in business and the professions have been feeling but unable to put words to. Most of the people I have talked to realize that they have come to some kind of transition in their lives. *Halftime* gave them a way to name what they are feeling. They tell me that the book has given them a new sense of opportunity, a change of season, a desire to adapt a new life more appropriate to the next season—it's like a watershed where all the landmarks change on the other side. There is a sense of adventure to it mixed with a fear of the unknown.

I am convinced that this feeling that seems to come as we approach midlife is broadly felt, and it is good. It is not something we should fear or deny. But I have also learned that not everyone who logs in a Halftime journey completes it, which is why I have written this book. I have listened to countless stories of those who started the journey but got stuck, and I have been able to help some of them get unstuck. In the following chapters you will learn about some of the false paths and false myths that lead you away from a Second Half of significance, and you will learn how to take advantage of the current economic boom to turn your Second Half dream into a reality.

It is not necessary for you to have read *Halftime* to make sense of this book, but it will help. In that book I walk you through a process of discovering how to plan and execute a Second Half that is characterized more by meaning and significance than by achievement. As one reader wrote, "I never dreamed that just one year [after reading *Halftime*]...I would be leaving my twenty-three year career in the corporate world." Over and over again I hear from people who read *Halftime* and have written to tell me it described perfectly where they were and prodded them to do something quite daring and unusual.

I have organized this book into three sections. The first deals with being stuck and why it's not the worst thing to happen to people on the journey into the Second Half of their lives. I will explore the dangers, fears, and dark sides of a too-long-extended period of Halftime.

In the second section I will begin to show you how to get unstuck. I will introduce you to some new tools and explain how there are new rules you must follow in the Second Half. I will also show you how this period of your life can be the harvest of your First Half's achievements and learning—a time for a hundred-fold impact on the world around you. I will explain why I think the Second Half is America's new frontier—an age of options and unprecedented opportunities brought on by the twentieth century's expansive economy and improvements in medical technology. As a result, you will probably live thirty years longer than your grandparents, and you will enjoy an affluence that would have been previously thought of as unimaginable.

The central feature of Section Two will be the Halftime Transition Toolbox, a set of disciplines, practices, and frameworks for looking at life that comes primarily from two sources: the hours and hours I have spent with the great wisdom figure in my life, Peter Drucker, and the simple but brilliant processes conceived by Dan Sullivan in his Strategic Coach program, which I consider the absolute best thing available for managing oneself *(www.strategiccoach.com).*

The third section will help you decide if you really want to make a change in your life. No one can make that decision for you, but I will provide you with information that will help you envision what a Second Half of significance will be like. Halftime is a place to be for a season, but more importantly it is a place to leave when its work is done. As people sometimes say about Manhattan, "It's a nice place to visit but I wouldn't want to live there." You can't stay in Halftime forever. You either go back to the way you lived the First Half of your life, or you change direction and head into the Second Half.

One critical factor for a successful Halftime is the need to share your hopes and dreams with someone else. I am pleased to report that my publisher recognized this and recently released a multimedia version of *Halftime* in one of their successful GroupWare kits. I strongly urge you to consider forming a small group at work or through your church and use this excellent resource to take you to the next step in making Halftime a productive and rewarding effort (see *www.Halftime.org*).

The filmmakers captured *very* provocative stories and the process almost facilitates conversation by itself.

Finally, you will notice that much of what I believe about our longing for significance comes from my Christian faith. I believe the desire to leave the world a better place than when you entered it comes from God. And yet, I have had friends who were not particularly religious or interested in spiritual things who have the same feelings and have used the Halftime model to make a transition in their careers toward significance. So if you are not yet able to accept the faith-oriented underpinnings to this book, I hope you will give it a try anyway. The basic principle, which cuts across all ideologies, is simply this: You are at your very best when you are investing yourself in others.

Bob Buford
Still Point Farm
June 2000

Section One

STUCK IN HALFTIME

ONE
BEYOND GOOD INTENTIONS

Halftime is a good place to go. It is not a good place to stay. It is a season—a place that gets increasingly uncomfortable if you make a career out of it, as some do.

Life is a series of tests. There are different trials for different seasons. Halftime is the trial that follows success—or, you might say, runs alongside success. It can also be the trial that follows the moment you say, "Enough of this!" Or after someone else says that for you. Halftime is that time when you have completed something and need to decide what to do next.

When I wrote my first book, *Halftime,* I hoped to see those who read it move from the success they had enjoyed in their careers to a Second Half of life filled with significance. I imagined thousands of people involved in new or parallel careers where they would be using their strengths and abilities to make the world better.

I have come to realize that most people are intrigued by the *idea* of a shift from success to significance, but this is new territory that they are reluctant to enter. And many who have chosen to enter, find the going tougher than they thought it would be.

Halftime feels good...for a while. People describe it as a sense of release. Success—which I define as doing reasonably well at your chosen career—has made huge demands on those who attain it, particularly in our hyper-competitive culture where conditions can change virtually overnight. First Half years are intense years: raising kids, solidifying a marriage (maybe two), making our mark at work, paying the bills. Life between the ages of twenty-something and forty-something is not easy. The combination of marriage, family, and career can be pretty consuming—which explains the appeal of Halftime. By the time most of us approach our fourth decade, anything that promises relief gets our attention.

It is the potential of that last deal—the decision to cut the ties and go for it—that brings a maelstrom of intense and often contradictory emotions: a mixture of joy and regret, freedom from the past and uncertainty about the future.

In my own case, when I finally sold my company—the company my mother had founded fifty-five years before, the company with my name on the door, the place where I spent my entire adult lifetime—the ending was surprisingly abrupt. The final event, as these things usually seem to be, was staged in a corporate law firm hermetically sealed from city sounds fifty-four floors above downtown Dallas. The quiet was eerie as investment bankers, lawyers, accountants, and venture capitalists moved almost ghostlike between conference rooms speaking in hushed confidential tones—as if noise might upset this delicate, finely calibrated transaction.

All the suspense that had been so palpable for months was coming to an end. I had been consigned to a small room to read the newspaper and wait. Earlier that morning, Kay Monigold, the highly capable Chief Administrative Officer of my company, Buford Television, Inc., had handed me a single slip of paper—one of those little notepads that always sit by the telephone in hotel rooms—which told me that we had just the night before achieved the number of cable subscribers required to close the transaction.

We all shook hands with that sort of wary congratulations that seem to be a feature of such events. I had a few words with the buyer, a leveraged-to-the-hilt forty-something cable tycoon whom I had known through the Young Presidents Organization. But I could tell I was already ancient history. He had work to do. And so did Kay Monigold and the other people I had worked so closely with for twenty years. They were committed to the new venture now, and there was a planning meeting that afternoon at a corporate retreat center near Austin.

Without me.

I had been promised a celebratory lunch that turned out to be oversized sandwiches wrapped in waxed paper. The only ones with me were Ben Hooks, the President of BTI who was also being bought out, and Pat Thompson, an investment banker for my side. We were assigned a windowless, unused conference room crowded with boxes of papers—probably from someone else's deal.

The others had to be on the road for Austin. They had targets to meet and the junk-bond holders and venture capitalists were hot on their heels. Not a moment to be lost between this closing and the soonest possible IPO.

Ben, Pat, and I reminisced a while. Then we said good-bye to the secretaries who were the only ones now remaining. That was it. My company had disappeared into another company. I was left with two things: the cash, and the rest of my life.

I imagined that this was how it must feel to be the last player to leave the arena after an NBA championship game. The spectators eventually file out through the corridors, find their cars, and drive home. The rest of the players and coaches have given the last interviews and are already thinking about the next season. The camera crews roll up their cables and head for the studio. And I'm still on the floor, taking it all in.

One season had ended and another was about to begin, and I had no idea how it would turn out. All I knew for sure was that I was not ready to jump back in the game and play it as I had the last one.

I was in Halftime…again. My first Halftime occurred several years before when I had made some significant changes in my life so that I could spend more time on work that reflected my core values. My Second Half career really developed into a parallel career where I was able to provide leadership for my business as well as start up Leadership Network, an organization that provides training and support for America's largest churches (to learn more, check our Website at *www.leadnet.org*). So I had a place to go and a mission in life that had long since eclipsed my business interests. Still, I felt considerable transition anxiety.

Halftime is that place where we can work out those feelings and find a clearer picture of the life we were intended to live.

From my own experience and the experiences of others, I have found that having a next step ready, even a partial one, helps. The best Halftime outcomes are those where people have begun a parallel career years earlier. For example, Alistair Hannah, a senior partner at McKinsey & Company, the international management consulting firm, spends several days a week leading Alpha, the hugely successful evangelism program now adopted by 1,700 churches in the United States, while maintaining his ties to

McKinsey. Frances Hesselbein paralleled her career as wife and mother with service to the Girl Scouts USA, stepping in time into the presidency of that organization and then becoming president of the Peter F. Drucker Foundation for Nonprofit Management *(www.pfdf.org)*, which has changed the way leaders think of their roles in nonprofits.

Bill Hybels, Rick Warren, and Robert Lewis are the senior pastors of hugely successful megachurches in Chicago, Orange County, and Little Rock. Each has begun a burgeoning parallel career to teach other churches the new approaches their churches have been so successful in pioneering. These efforts will almost certainly provide the focal points for the Second Half of these men's lives, as has been the case for John Maxwell, the best-selling author, speaker, and leader in the leadership development field. Wally Hawley, the founder of InterWest, a vibrant Silicon Valley venture capital firm, began in his fifties to invest himself—his time, his money, his skills as a board member—in a portfolio of good works initiatives that will pay off in changed lives.

But these cases aren't the norm. The story I hear most often is "Bob, I'm stuck in Halftime," which is why I'm writing this book. It's a book for people who have completed, or know at some point they will complete, the First Half of their lives with a winning season—perhaps not undefeated, but more wins than losses and maybe a few championship years. (The venture capitalists who bought my company brought out an IPO less than six months later valued at double their investment—money I apparently left on the table!) Some of these people read *Halftime,* resonated with its message, even started exploring some Second Half ideas, only to get stuck in the locker room. I've run into more than a few who say, "I still don't know what I'm going to do next. I feel like I'm stuck."

For example, there's John Castle, a brilliant lawyer (first in his class at the University of Texas at Austin Law School) who was a founding partner in a huge corporate firm in Dallas and went on to become executive vice president for Electronic Data Systems, the company that Ross Perot founded. He played a leading role on the team that crafted the separation of EDS from General Motors, formed a new board, and recruited a new CEO. Financially secure, John says, "I'm still not sure what comes next." A person of deep faith and values, John wants to serve but still hasn't found his place. He's in limbo. He's surprised that Halftime is taking so long and wondering whether he will ever be committed again with the sort of energy his First Half manifested.

Then there's Frank Ashton, who built a group of natural foods grocery stores in California, selling out at age forty-something to Whole Earth Foods. The last time I saw Frank, several months ago and several years after the sale, he said, "I'm dabbling." But I sensed he wanted to be doing more.

Jim Wilson has been riding the ups and downs of the real estate business in the superhot markets of Denver and Atlanta. Currently he's up. A person with movie-star good looks, Jim had a profound religious conversion several years ago at a Foundation Conference. He has wondered ever since what that might mean to his Second Half if he could ever walk away from the real estate business. He's made plenty of money, but like Peggy Lee in her Grammy-winning song, Jim is asking, "Is this all there is?" Now he's at a turning point and he's stuck. What now? What next? Not sure.

Being wealthy helps, but there are also a lot of people like Tim, a teacher who was recently offered an opportunity to retire early (he's fifty) with a sizable cash pension. He refused. Tim has always looked forward to not having to report to a classroom five days a week so that he could try his hand at some entrepreneurial activities he'd been cooking up. He knows he has at least another twenty-five years of "active duty." He has always wanted to start a consulting firm to help companies hire and train at-risk youth, and now he appears to have that chance. He turned down the offer this year, but next year will be his last chance to accept it. He's not sure what to do. The security of a weekly paycheck, uncertainty over whether he will miss the one-on-one contact he has with students, and a general anxiety about leaving a profession all weigh heavily on Tim's mind. He's immobilized with indecision. He's done all the right things I suggested in *Halftime,* and he's even worked through most of the activities and inventories in my second book, *Game Plan.* But he just can't get going.

I am writing this book with Jim and Frank and John and Tim in mind. But I am also writing it for you. If you have read *Halftime* yet still aren't sure how you will spend your Second Half, or even if you have not read that book but sense that you really can't live the Second Half of your life the way you did the first but you're not sure what to do about it, then this book is especially for you.

It is meant to be useful, not just interesting. I want to help you get unstuck. To move from good intentions to results; from latent energy to active energy; from faith alone to works of service; from a life of benign comfort to one of commitment and the discomfort that always goes with renewed ambition.

———

Most of us have a deep need to make a difference, to leave the world a better place. For people of faith, working to please our great Creator God is a major motive for making the Second Half count. When we come to the end of our lives, standing before God to give an account of what we did with what we were given, we want to hear, "Well done my good and faithful servant," not "So what?"

Many people have successfully left Halftime and are enjoying a Second Half that they say is the richest and best season of their lives. Wally Hawley, my recovering venture capitalist friend, told me a few days ago: "People have it backwards. Most people worry about what they will sacrifice in their Second Half. The sacrifice is in the First Half—the travel, the stress, the triviality of so much of it. The Second Half is where the joy is." It may not be conventional wisdom, but it is absolutely true.

You may have started a few years back and now find yourself stuck trying to figure out just what to do with the next thirty years of your life. Or this may be your first venture into Halftime. Regardless of where you are right now, this book will help get you moving in the right direction—right into the most exciting journey of your life.

TWO
STUCK IS GOOD

A man doesn't grow old because he has lived a certain number of years, he grows old when he deserts his ideals.

Gen. Douglas MacArthur

Often the phone will ring, and a voice on the other end will say, "You don't know me, but my name is Steve. I read your book, and it really got me thinking. I realize I'm in Halftime, but I don't have a clue what I'm going to do next. Could we get together and talk about it?"

I've heard this plea over and over almost verbatim. The stories are different, but the bottom line is the same: "I'm stuck in Halftime." I almost feel guilty about prompting a movement that a lot of people seem unable to finish. Almost, but not quite, for Halftime is really inevitable, and ultimately—if you are serious about it—you will find your way into the most exciting twenty to thirty years of your life. If you get stuck along the way toward figuring out what you will do with the rest of your life, that's not so bad. It means you are asking the right questions. Your Second Half can be filled with adventure. But adventure always means uncertainty. No risk. No adventure.

If we just look at demographics, the First Half has pretty much come to an end for that huge group of

Americans we call Baby Boomers. If you are in your forties or early fifties, you are in Halftime whether you realize it or not. If you are in your thirties and have enjoyed a degree of success or accomplishment, you are probably in Halftime too. But Halftime is not just an issue of age. It's more an issue of transitions. A business has been sold. Your marital status has changed. You've gone broke. Or suddenly gotten rich. You find yourself with more free time than ever before. Something inside says you cannot keep doing what you do. I'm not sure it really matters what the triggering event is. Something in your life has changed, placing you in that in-between state—that fluid state I call Halftime.

Many people think that acknowledging they are in Halftime is enough. While it is a step in the right direction to admit you have reached the end of a season in your life—a critical step—there's just not enough purposeful-ness in such an admission to make a permanent Halftime a satisfying way to live. You may leave the all-out inten-sity of your First Half work, but an early retirement to a life of leisure with maybe some community service thrown in on the side is not likely to satisfy people who are purpose driven. The purpose doesn't have to be com-mercial activity but you must have a reason to get up in the morning.

One of the benefits of getting stuck in Halftime is that it forces you to ask more questions; to dig deeper into what you are looking for and how to find it. It can compel you to get serious about knowing who you are designed to be and discovering how to live closer to who you really are. Most of the people with whom I've talked have entered Halftime with too much optimism or idealism. They assumed that all they needed was a few days or weeks to choose a new career, and then they would just get on with it. This is really just a continuation of First

Half behavior—the typical success-oriented approach to life. Let's face it, if you have been working sixty hours a week for twenty years, just about any change looks good. It did not take much arm-twisting to convince you it was time to survey your life, dream about where you would like to be in ten years, line up your priorities, and get going again. It sounded good at first, but like any good thing, it was hard work, and it took longer than you thought it would.

I don't think any of us realize just how hard it is to make the transition from a success-driven life to one whose primary focus is significance. It is more than a shift from one job to another, but a change in your entire mindset. It requires not only periods of honest and sometimes painful reflection but the willingness to take some chances that may lead nowhere. For example, you may think that your Second Half career will involve working with teenagers, but when you volunteer to spend a few hours mentoring teens at a local agency, you realize this is not how you are wired. That has a way of stopping you in your tracks and making you wonder if this Halftime thing is really what you need. Trust me, it is.

When you run into these barricades along the way, the tendency is to either put things in neutral or just go back to your hard-charging former self. Instead, you need to expect these barriers as a logical and natural result of your Halftime experience. It means you are taking this adventure seriously, and it serves as a helpful signal to let you know you're either heading in the wrong direction or you're not asking yourself the right questions. Getting stuck is a good reminder of something you've known all your adult life and that author M. Scott Peck repeated in his best-selling book *The Road Less Traveled:* Life isn't easy.

WHAT DID YOU EXPECT?

In many ways, Halftime is like marriage and raising a family. You go into it somewhat idealistic, and then somewhere along the line you discover that it's hard. It's hard to find the right spouse among all those people you went to college with. It's hard and in many ways unforgiving to raise children. And yet, it also brings great joy and fulfillment, which is why many parents experience an emptiness and sense of loss when their children grow up and move out on their own. All along we think being free of the responsibility of children will give us more free time for our leisure pursuits. But we learn that going from breakneck speed with countless challenges to a very quiet house is not as fulfilling as we thought it would be.

In fact, one of the most frequent reasons for people getting stuck in Halftime is that they were expecting leisure to fulfill them.

Halftime is not about leisure. If you want leisure, take a long vacation and do nothing until you get tired of it. Believe me, you will get tired of it. Author Mihaly Csikszentmihalyi has conducted landmark studies on what makes people happy (see his book *Flow: The Psychology of Optimal Experience*). One of the things he has learned from years of research on the subject is that leisure and "free time" is *not* what makes us happy or content. Real happiness comes when we have a specific goal and are engaged in meeting that goal. If we lose sight of the goal, we drift back to boredom. If the goal is too big and unattainable, we give up. We are at our best when we are in that zone between anxiety and boredom. Csikszentmihalyi calls this the "flow zone," and it explains why within a year or two after their injuries, quadriplegics return to their original level of happiness—the same with lottery winners. We are wired to be engaged in meaningful activities most of our lives, and Halftime is a deliberate and strategic effort to stay engaged but with the right things.

If you go into Halftime thinking it will be easy or that you will emerge with a plan to spend the rest of your life in leisure, you will get discouraged. You will have taken yourself out of the flow zone—out of your natural rhythm—and wonder why you aren't making any progress. Leisure is important, but it should not be the sole focus of your Halftime journey. If you find yourself stuck in Halftime, take a closer look at how you're spending your time. If most of your days are spent on the golf course or a boat or traveling (some of the most common venues for Halftimers), go back to the drawing board—literally. Review "what's in the box" (the single motivating force in your life). Ask yourself where you really want to be in ten years. What you're really good at. And how you can turn those skills and knowledge into a new enterprise that contributes to others.

TRIED IT, DIDN'T WORK

Another reason people get stuck in Halftime is what I call the "all-or-none syndrome." They get jazzed about walking away from a successful career and expect to jump right into a "significant career" overnight. At least that's the expectation I've sensed in many I've talked with.

Charles (not his real name) was a successful CEO in the communications field when he began to feel the pull of significance. He had worked his way up literally from the bottom of his company, which has offices in thirty states. Long hours combined with a real savvy for management put him at the top before his forty-fifth birthday, and between his salary, bonuses, and stock options, he realized money was no longer a motivator for him. When approached by a friend to take a position in a completely different career from the one in which he had spent nearly twenty-five years, he jumped at the opportunity, thinking it would fill the void he was feeling. But after a year, it was clear that this type of work was just not for him. It has been six years since he left, and he's still not sure what to do next. He serves on a couple of boards and plays a lot of tennis, but in terms of transferring his incredible skills to work for which he is passionate, it just isn't happening.

Charles made the mistake, I believe, of jumping too fast into something foreign and unfamiliar from what he had been doing for his entire adult life. He severed his ties with a company and an industry in which he was held in high esteem, and now he waits for his phone to ring. This is a common pitfall for people who are eager to make the transition from success to significance, which is why I think one of the best ways to explore a Second Half career is to first embark on a serious parallel career.

When I was in my forties, I knew I wanted to eventually leave the cable television business and devote myself entirely to my personal mission, which is to turn the latent energy in American Christianity into active energy. But for a lot of reasons, I was not yet ready to abruptly sever the ties with my business. So I renegotiated my working arrangement with the company so that I could develop a parallel career, which was the founding and oversight of Leadership Network, an organization that serves the nation's most successful pastors and churches.

This career that ran alongside my "day job" gave me a chance to see if I could translate my skills and knowledge gained in business into the unique environment of the nonprofit. Just because you were successful in one particular area does not guarantee that you will be as successful in another. Most (but not all) Second Half careers will place you in roles that use skills that are not dissimilar to the ones with which you have made your mark in the First Half, even though the context may be different.

By developing a parallel career instead of just leaving the cable business and moving full time into Leadership Network, I gave myself something of a safety net in case things didn't work out. For those who will need *some* income source, this can be a significant reason for trying a parallel career (although I can't think of a single case where the shift from success to significance was accompanied by serious financial hardship—money really *isn't* everything).

Finally, because things eventually *did* work out, it confirmed that inner voice that seemed to be leading me into the nonprofit sector, and this may be the biggest benefit of developing a parallel career. It is yet another way to help you discover where you really belong. Sometimes a parallel career will not work at all, which is a tremendously valuable experience. It's sort of like an internship where you work alongside a surgeon and decide you don't really want to be a surgeon, a blessed revelation to future patients as well as to the intern.

It is not a bad thing to be stuck. It means that you are taking your journey seriously. You may have expected Halftime to be easier. You may have jumped too early into a Second Half career. Regardless of the cause, you now find yourself back in that uncomfortable world of in-between. And tempted to go back to your First Half way of life.

It could be that you are really suffering from a toxic addiction.

THREE

DETOXING FROM THE ADDICTION TO SUCCESS

The rich man...is always sold to the institution which makes him rich....

Why should we be in such desperate haste to succeed and in such desperate enterprises? If a man does not keep pace with his companions, perhaps it is because he hears a different drummer. Let him step to the music which he hears, however measured or far away.

Henry David Thoreau

Success is addictive. Like a drug, it never completely satisfies. No matter how much you have, it is never enough.

For the most part I have found success to be a positive addiction, but like all good things, it can go toxic. After a certain point it takes control of your life. Henry David Thoreau describes in *Walden* a situation where one becomes "possessed by his possessions"; where "the cows become the masters of the farmers."

That is what success can do to you.

Peter Drucker told me this same idea in two words. It was early in our relationship at a time when I was in hot pursuit of my corporate growth goals (in the first twelve years of my presidency of Buford Television, Inc., we grew at 28 percent a year compound annual rate). It was late in the afternoon at the end of a long and profitable day. I said, "I think most people would give their left arm to be where I am." Peter said, "I wouldn't." I have never forgotten that moment.

Somewhere along the way, people who have achieved a level of success—whether it be financial or otherwise—get caught up in the thrill of the chase, the pressure of deadlines, the exhilaration of doing important things for seemingly high stakes. And in many ways it is simpler to focus mindlessly and fully on a single objective. Here's what Bobby Haas, a Dallas megadeal maker told *The Dallas Morning News* as he transitioned to a life increasingly focused on his family and more socially responsible interests:

> I found out that leading a balanced life is more challenging than being a workaholic. Once I was a race car driver in the Indianapolis 500; now I'm an acrobat walking a tightrope.
>
> When you pursue one goal, you do so in a madcap way. You must focus on the road, go at maximum speed. You can't think about anything else.

It's just natural for speed racers like Haas to focus all their energy on staying ahead of the other fast guys.

We secretly, or not so secretly, enjoy comparing ourselves to others who aren't moving at quite the same pace. It's not that we intentionally try to lord it over others, not at all. It's all part of the need to measure success, and one of the ways to do that is to look around to see where the competition is. You need to know you are ahead, and even though you inwardly know that making a lot of money or holding a prestigious position is not what gives you worth, you still get deluded into thinking it does. You begin to believe your own press releases.

Success is not bad. It is a good thing to have worked hard and accomplished much. If you need heart bypass surgery, there is nothing noble about seeking the unsuccessful surgeon who happens to be your brother-in-law to try to fix your heart. You want the best and will be thankful that the medical profession rewards success. The abundance of good things we enjoy in our culture is largely a result of the drive for success. We are beneficiaries of our immigrant forefathers who came here penniless and through hard work and the desire to get ahead built great enterprises in industry, education, medicine, science, and the like. And we are right to follow their example. Max Weber, the eminent sociologist, even saw through to the religious underpinnings of what he called the "Protestant Work Ethic."

So it is important to recognize that the desire to move from success to significance is not a criticism of success but the recognition that success is a season. True, it is exciting; intoxicating—literally. It is a good place to be. It is not an easy place to leave, but when it's time, it's time.

Ken Blanchard knew that it was time. Ken has known great success. The coauthor of several best-selling books, including *The One Minute Manager,* Ken has sold more than nine million books. He and his brilliant and attractive wife, Margie, began Blanchard Training and Development fifteen or so years ago and built it into one of the leading management training organizations in the world. He has made a life of speaking to big (and admiring) audiences all over the country. He writes books that are always in demand. He leads satellite-delivered teleconferences all over the world. Ken and Margie are riding a wonderful wave of success that feels like it could go on forever, and it has been a great ride.

Ken is sixty, as I am. A few years ago he began hearing that still, small voice in his inner life. A wise man, Ken listened. He sensed that despite all that he had accomplished, there was something more, just out of his reach, and it had nothing to do with growing his business bigger. He knew what he wanted to do, but first, he says, he had to admit he had an addiction problem. He needed to detox from success. He needed to free himself from its power. You do not spend half of your life being told how great you are without developing a dependency on such accolades. Ken freely admits that success breeds ego, and for him, ego means we Edge God Out. We put ourselves rather than God at the center of our lives. Once he admitted to himself that he was addicted to success, he could begin dealing with his addiction. Now Ken has redeployed his great gift by teaching people how to lead their businesses as if their faith mattered. He founded the FaithWalk Leadership Center and is tremendously energized about the next decade of his life and beyond.

You do not have to be a world-class management guru to be afflicted with the addiction to success. If you started out selling insurance, you soon experienced the thrill of leading your area in sales for the month, only to set your sights on becoming the top salesman of the year. You may be in middle management; you understand the drive to always make your budget, contribute to your company's profits, or turn out quality products in an efficient manner. Success begets success. It also attracts attention so that top salespeople become regional managers, who then may be set out on their own and parlay their equity and skills into entrepreneurship.

There is nothing wrong with being the best, but it becomes an addiction when our desire to win causes us to not have time for our God, our wives, our families and friends, or to put something meaningful back into our communities. Being the best can be a jealous mistress—it does not leave time for much else because it is so hard to say no to that early morning breakfast meeting, the next trip, the dinner with clients. While it is more socially acceptable to be addicted to success, it can be just as damaging as alcohol, drugs, or a mistress.

The American Dream is a wonderful thing, but at some point we wake up. We know we can't continue at the same level of intensity, but despite our attempts to find a more meaningful and significant Second Half career, the siren song of success pulls us back into the fray.

Many people who enter Halftime eventually go back to their First Half lives because they miss the thrill of the chase. They need another fix of success. As Dallas businessman Bill Custard once told me, "The problem is we don't have another way of measuring our self-worth."

Tom Wolfe is a modern master of the great sprawling novel that describes a whole culture. Some critics say Wolfe is the successor to Balzac in this genre of book. I flew from Tyler to Dallas several years ago seated next to Wolfe—decked out in his signature white linen suit. It was just after the release of *Bonfire of the Vanities,* the hugely successful novel describing Wall Street "masters of the universe," high and low society in Manhattan. He was beginning to work on a new novel about the real estate business *(A Man in Full)* that was to consume the next eleven years of his life. I suggested a few of my real estate friends in Dallas, and one of them made it into the book (but that's another story).

The central characters in these two books that captured my attention for hours on end both portray the evanescence of success. Charlie Croaker of *A Man in Full* is an aging Georgia Tech football legend with a legacy of bad knees. Charlie is immensely proud of his manly physical appearance ("a man in full with the neck of a Jersey bull"). In the flush of success as the book begins—custom appointed jet, 26,000-acre plantation, beautiful and young trophy wife, palatial house in the tony suburb of Buckhead—Charlie has all the trappings of success.

What stands out in both books is how quickly it all fades for the successful main characters—Charlie in *A Man in Full* and Sherman McCoy, the Park Avenue bond trader in *Bonfire of the Vanities*. Sooner or later they came to the realization—as we all do—that things have inevitably and irretrievably changed. There is no pathway back to the former success state, even if we crave it.

"Planned abandonment" (that's what Peter Drucker calls it) is necessary to clear the decks for the next stage. It is amazing to me how closely Thoreau captured the spirit of today's successful suburbanite when he wrote:

> The mass of men lead lives of quiet desperation. What is called resignation is confirmed desperation. From the desperate city you go into the desperate country, and have to console yourself with the bravery of minks and muskrats. A stereotyped but unconscious despair is concealed even under what are called the games and amusements of mankind. There is no play in them, for this comes after work. But it is a characteristic of wisdom not to do desperate things.

The CEO of an Internet provider once said to a friend of mine, "We'd really love to sell our big house and buy a small one in the country and go back to doing what we really love." Sound familiar? The sad irony is that nothing is stopping him from doing that. Nothing, that is, except an addiction to a lifestyle that reflects his success.

The good news is that you *can* regain control of your life. But it will be hard. You will initially miss the very busyness you are trying to escape. And you will also come to learn that Halftime has an unpleasant side with which you also must deal.

FOUR

THE FALSE PATHS OF HALFTIME

In the age of ultraprosperity, it's easy to make a dollar, but hard to make a difference.
Kevin Kelly

Success is nice and I've had some and enjoyed it, but so what? We're all running around being busy and doing important things but this has nothing to do with anything. Up there God and the angels are looking down and laughing, and not unkindly. They just find us touching and dizzy.

Peggy Noonan

I have a major concern about these next two chapters. My fear is that you will read them and get discouraged. Or worse, that you will remain stuck in Halftime and maybe abandon this whole journey altogether before you get to Sections Two and Three where all the good stuff is.

Each season of life is a series of trials, and Halftime is no exception. When I introduce people to the idea of Halftime, they seem to "get it" immediately and are eager to begin working on their own positive transition experience. They understand the need to make a change in their lives, and for the first time they see this change as something positive rather than a crisis. But there are aspects of Halftime that pose serious problems that can derail you if you are not prepared for them. If you need to, skip over these next two chapters, but I think it is helpful to see the obstacles on the Halftime journey and thus be in a better position to overcome them.

In many ways, Halftime is like crossing a jungle clearing that contains a series of deep pits camouflaged with coverings of leaves and grass. You have just emerged from years of fighting your way through the brush, and that clearing looks so inviting. Finally, the sun is shining and you have a much clearer view of your destination. But as you race across the smooth, unobstructed landscape, you stand a good chance of falling into one of these deep holes, never to be seen again, at least in the land of significance.

I no longer wonder that it is a relatively small percentage of people who successfully make the transition from success to significance. The temptation to stop when you fall into one of these "holes" is logical, normal, and predictable. Yet to my way of thinking, normal is never enough. Normalcy is what Kierkegaard calls "artificial hell." Once you catch a glimpse of what your Second Half could be, going back isn't an acceptable option. But staying in the pit is just as bad.

Many people back out of Halftime because they fear that as soon as they stop doing what has made them successful, they will lose *their* significance. It's that huge, unspoken fear we all have of being a "nobody." On the day after Steve Wynn made a deal to merge his Las Vegas gambling empire (The Venetian, The Bellagio, etc.) with that of his arch competitor, Kirk Kekorian, the *Wall Street Journal*'s headline referred to Wynn in the *past tense.* Overnight, this major player—most people considered

Wynn the innovation leader in his industry—seemed to go, at least in the eyes of the media, from Mr. Legendary to Mr. Used-to-Be.

This is a major issue for all of us. Every person needs to be a hero—needs to be needed, needs to be affirmed, needs to be acknowledged. We need to know that we count, and in our current culture, "counting" usually includes a title, a business card, an office in a recognizable business. Whatever your role in your present position, you have reasonable expectations of being valued, hopefully by the entire company, but at least by those who report to you. You hope that your absence would be felt, and something about that gives us all a real charge. When it gets right down to it, one real fear that prevents people from working through Halftime is the possibility that if they leave their First Half life, people won't need them anymore.

I think that is why we are so vulnerable to at least two false paths that look so promising when we are in midlife. The first is the path that leads us back home. It is the one that says the status quo is not really all that bad after all. The second false path is the one that promises leisure. It tells you that after working so hard during the First Half of your life you deserve a break. Both paths take us far from the real adventure that is ours when we commit to doing something truly significant with our lives.

Which destination looks like the place you want to spend the rest of your life?

THE HOMESTEAD

Most people who begin to feel as if they need to make a major change in their lives never really make it into the Second Half. They might spend some time daydreaming about a new and exciting career that matches their talents with that growing sense of mission, but eventually they give up and stick to what they have been doing all along. They're like those people who always talk about moving to a new house but end up staying in the old homestead forever. Many who have made an inner commitment to move from success to significance have gone back to success. It's just too easy to stay where it's comfortable, familiar, *especially* when we choose a Halftime track that is idealistic but not quite grounded in reality.

Walt Wilson, a Silicon Valley entrepreneur and a Leadership Network Board member, puts it this way: "I find so many people I know in the Valley who have read *Halftime* and prayed about it, but I see them drifting back to business; back to making money again."

A few years ago a friend of mine invited me to join him for lunch. He had just turned fifty at the time and when we met in my office, secure behind a closed door, he told me that he had been praying for three weeks about an important decision he had to make. He sought me out because he knew I had faced a similar decision, and he wanted to hear how I went about choosing what I did.

My friend, whom I will call Frank, is a very capable businessman. A natural leader with a lot of capacity, he had risen through the ranks of his company in record time. Now he was at the threshold. He explained that he was recently offered the top job in the company, but the opportunity was coming at a time when he had been thinking of pursuing options that had more to do with significance than success.

I explained to Frank the concept of a parallel career—how he might be able to negotiate a work arrangement that would allow him to develop a "significance career" alongside his corporate work. Often this is the best way to test the waters in your Halftime journey, but in Frank's case, it wasn't an option. His company was asking for a five-year commitment that would be very demanding, involve a lot of travel, and require his full attention. The payoff, however, was attractive: a mega-salary coupled with great stock options. Already Frank was financially comfortable, but if he accepted the promotion, in five years he would be able to retire with more than enough money to do what he pleased the rest of his life.

I asked Frank what his other option was and he explained that he really wanted to go to seminary and train to become a minister. He felt that he could apply his leadership skills to running a large church but that he needed the seminary degree in order to have the "credentials" to become a senior minister somewhere.

After he laid out the pros and cons of both options, he asked me what I thought he should do.

"I think you've already decided," I responded. "You're going to take the promotion." Which he did.

Five years later he exited the company, just as he had planned, with a generous supply of money. He still had a strong desire to give something back; to engage himself in something of lasting and significant value. But the five years had taken their toll. He tried working with a seminary. He established a relationship with a denomination. He worked with a parachurch group. His expertise had been in the area of reengineering—tear a company down, take it apart, and reconstruct it into a leaner, more efficient organization. But none of the religious groups he tried to work with were interested in that.

Frank got discouraged and started looking for other things to do. He was a young fifty-five, wealthy and talented, with a lot of time on his hands and the need to do something important. He became a partner in a venture capital fund. Did a little teaching in business schools. Did some traveling. What he was doing amounted to a pleasant and nondemanding portfolio of activities, but no real sense of mission. No driving passion. It's what my friend, Tom Tierney, chairman of the worldwide consulting firm Bain & Co. said he saw so many retired corporate executives doing. He called it "sanctioned dabbling." It doesn't produce a significant outcome but everyone affirms it.

Frank had decided by default against making a major commitment. He had set up a straw man: seminary vs. CEO. Not much of a choice, really. If he were faced with a decision inside his company, he would have gotten a lot more information and explored many more options. Instead, he made the tragic but common mistake of thinking the only way you can make a significant contribution in life is to become a fully ordained minister in a big church. Given such a choice, it was inevitable that he would stay with his company.

Many who hear the still, small voice urging them to leave success for significance never make the leap because the inertia of their work is too strong to escape. They genuinely want to try something new and exciting, but they give themselves such unrealistic options that staying put becomes the only real choice they have. Like Frank, so many of us find we need to stay just a few years longer, accumulate just a little more wealth before we can "comfortably" make the leap into significance.

Frank's story parallels so many that I have heard from people who considered the leap from success to significance. They begin to lose their passion for making money and achieving. Their instincts—which I believe may be the voice of God—are right. There is so much more to life than accumulation, whether it be money, titles, or toys.

There's a biblical parallel in the story of the rich young ruler. Jesus knew exactly why the rich young ruler came to him. He wanted to be saved, but he didn't know from what. Jesus knew that despite his wealth, he was empty. To be saved—which is the ultimate in significance—he had to rely on something other than wealth.

The rich young ruler (see Matthew 19) left Jesus a sad man, and we never know for sure what he did. Many people want significance but return to their First Half lives in sadness. They sense that the way to be saved from the addictions of the First Half is to respond to a call to serve others. But the pull of gravity is just too strong. They stick with what they know. They can't leave home.

LEISURE WORLD

Not everyone who gets stuck in Halftime goes back into the First Half. Many opt for what I call "Leisure World." The life you thought you always wanted. No morning commute. Golf whenever you feel like it. Pack up and travel anytime you get the urge. It is the traditionally held view of how the American Dream will pan out. Work hard, move up the ladder of success, then cash out and enjoy life before you're too old to do all those things you dreamed about.

If you are absolutely honest, you admit that the notion of being able to quit your job and spend the rest of your life doing whatever you wanted to do *is* pretty attractive. But leaving your First Half career for a life of leisure is probably the biggest mistake—and potentially the most deceitful false path—of Halftime. The downside is so unexpected (I will say a little more about that in the next chapter).

Listen to this story from a friend in Florida:

THE WAGES OF BOREDOM

Rogers Kirven was about to cash out his successful business. It would have given him enough money so that he would never have to work for the rest of his life. Rogers had worked extremely hard to get to this enviable position, and he wanted to reward himself. He envisioned the life of his dreams: more time with his wife and family, never having to start each day with a trip to the office, and most of all, freedom.

The day was almost there when all he had to do was sign his name and he would have enough cash to do whatever he wanted for the rest of his life. For some reason, just before he was to close the deal he decided to celebrate with two longtime buddies who had sold *their* companies a few years earlier. They met at a restaurant in Washington, D.C., and very soon into the conversation Rogers began to get nervous.

"The first thing they told me was that they had new wives," Kirven said. "I'd known one of them for fifteen years; the other for seven years. Both of them had cashed out to spend more time with their families!"

The conversation never got much beyond their toys and leisure activities, and the more they talked, the more terrified Rogers became. Instead of being excited about their lives, they seemed confused and disconnected, still wondering what to do with their lives. "There was a creeping sensation of 'Uh oh! Something has happened to my friends,'" Kirven said.

On the way out of the restaurant, Rogers was still looking for confirmation from them that cashing out to Leisure World was the best thing they had ever done. But when he asked one of the guys, an active Christian, that exact question, all he got in return was, "I don't know. I don't know."

Rogers decided to track down every person he could find who in search of a better life had cashed in seeking relief from First Half pressures. When last I talked to him, he had found and interviewed thirty-six men who, between the ages of forty and fifty, had turned their businesses into at least $5 million. This certainly isn't a statistically projectable sample, but I find it at the very least, an interesting and instructive window into the American Dream. How did it turn out?

"The first three guys I talked to were just like me," Rogers told me. "They loved God, loved their families, and were in the same age bracket, forty-two, forty-three, forty-four. They all had a strategy. They wanted to spend more time with their families and develop their own souls.

"Within a year all three were divorced. All three blew at least $1 million on new toys—bigger boat, bigger car, bigger plane. They all thought they had a solid game plan, but like Mike Tyson said about his boxing foes, 'They all had a strategy until they got hit.' Each of these guys stepped into a stream, and they didn't realize the current was so strong until they got swept away."

Of the thirty-six guys he interviewed, a remarkable thirty-two got divorced! All of them locked their targets on a new toy or affair but experienced tremendous depression after "acquiring" each new thing. What seemed like paradise turned out to be just the opposite. These guys tried what most of us would say is the ideal arrangement. Money is no object. You don't have to go to work. You can travel, play, and buy all you want. And instead of waiting until these guys were too old to enjoy their freedom, they did it while they were quite young. Somehow, it just didn't pan out the way they thought it would.

Compare these Leisure World citizens with a number of extremely wealthy people who were featured in the *Boston Globe* because despite not having to work, that's exactly what they did. People like Robert Gamble, of the Procter & Gamble family who, despite inheriting a fortune, works as a $25 an hour nurse-practitioner. As an article in the *Economist* (June 17, 2000) said:

> "Part of wanting to work is the Protestant work ethic, I guess," says Gamble. "But working is also what links you to other people. It's a way of being connected."
>
> Or consider someone like J. Stuart Moore whose stake in the publicly owned company that he founded is more than $1 billion. The thirty-eight-year-old father of five would never have to work another day in his life, yet he still goes to work every day. Why? "A life of leisure isn't a meaningful life. It isn't a satisfying life."

Robert Fogel, a Nobel Prize winning economist who says he approaches his subject from a totally secular point of view, writes in his book, *The Fourth Great Awakening*, about a sense of deprivation in modern American society. The deprivation that now worries him, however, is "spiritual" by which he means not only religious faith but a deprivation of such qualities as "self esteem, a sense of family, a sense of discipline, an appreciation of quality and–most important of all, he thinks–*a sense of purpose.*"

Once people have enough to eat, these qualities seem to Fogel to matter more than yet more material wealth.

As popular author Alex Comfort once wrote, "Leisure is a con." It promises far more than it delivers.

Leisure World is that place where all you do is go to dull dinners and talk about the last country you visited. It feels like it's going to be great. It's the place all the magazines advertise. The good life. No more worries. Cruise ship fantasy. It is a place, an experience, the next new thing. But it is not a life.

Jesus warned about treasures that eventually rust or fade, additional property that makes no incremental contribution. Sadly, the people who trade being stuck in Halftime for Leisure World often find it to be like a false front movie set. It looks great in the pictures, but it is not real behind the scenes.

KEEPING YOUR DREAM AHEAD OF YOU

Never, never, never let your dream get behind you. That's a dangerous place for it to be. And it happens all the time in the Second Half. There's some kind of tipping point where life begins to slide downhill into reminiscence. It's a comfortable feeling. You feel that your best days are behind you. The pressure is off. You have that great moment—now beyond the reach of risk and uncertainty—captured in a treasured photograph, a newspaper clipping. Those were the good days! And the farther the "good days" get into the past of faded photographs, the more they grow in remembrance. You imagine that life will never be as happy again as that shining moment.

Don't let this happen to you! I keep thinking that the best season of my life is the one I am in and the one just ahead, and it usually turns out that way. But I must have a dream that draws me forward. To lose a dream is to lose forward momentum, to live in the past. I want to never be captured by the past, my bad past or my good past. For a relentless dreamer, it isn't the outcome of the dream that counts; it's the dream itself.

Scott Fitzgerald, the American novelist, somehow lost his dream early. "Scott died inside himself at around the age of thirty or thirty-five" wrote Ernest Hemingway to his editor Max Perkins a year after Fitzgerald's death at age forty-four, "and his creative powers died somewhat later."

When I embarked on my Second Half career, I thought I would try and work a lot more leisure into my life. I thought I would be working four days a week at my office in Dallas and spending three at my farm where I am my most creative. I would also spend one week each month traveling or learning something new. Leisure with a purpose, but leisure just the same.

I think those are reasonable expectations for a Second Half, but it just has not worked out that way for me, and the reason is that meaningful work ultimately is more appealing than leisure. I could easily take more time off for leisure pursuits, but I'm enjoying what I'm doing too much. In most ways, it is the most exciting adventure I've ever had in my life.

A purposeful Second Half is that place where work, meaning, and happiness merge. It is where you can be fully engaged in activities that match your skills, capacity, and mission. We were meant to work, but so much of what we have done in the First Half was drudgery—necessary busyness that contributed to the bottom line but did not always reflect who we really were. It wasn't the work that was the problem, but the emptiness of much of it.

The answer is not to quit working but to find work that adds meaning and purpose to your life. One of the greatest adventures you can ever experience comes when you begin to invest your whole self into something that counts, something that lasts beyond now. When you find that place, you won't want to leave it.

Rogers Kirven was lucky. He swerved from Leisure World at the last minute. I asked him what others can do to avoid the trauma that those thirty-two men faced. Here's what he told me:

- *Don't be too anxious to quit your job!* Work is healthier than you think.
- *Pursue a peer group.* Not just any group, but a true peer group with people who are in the

same situation that you are in. Go for regular interaction and accountability.

- *Find a meaningful and significant lateral move to make before you leave what you're doing.* Once you experience that doing work for God is as thrilling and exciting as your regular work, you won't be so tempted to Leisure World.
- *Establish the right goals.* Ask yourself, "How can I build character goals, attitudes, and perspectives that will keep me from shipwreck like the others?"

Obviously, a life filled with purpose is ultimately more appealing than staying put or heading to Leisure World. And yet, look how easy it is to follow those two false paths. But in addition to these wrong turns you might make on your journey, you might also fall victim to some very unhelpful mythology.

FIVE

THE MYTHS OF HALFTIME

The god thou servest is thine own appetite.
Christopher Marlowe's *Dr. Faust*

Myths are important. Myths are the way we simplify our lives of impossible complexity into themes we can comprehend and live by. We read stories, see motion pictures, watch the evening news, absorbing thousands of media images (three thousand advertising impressions a day and the Internet is barely started!), go to church—and out of that we develop the simple, profound mental themes that inform who we are and where we belong. These myths help us shape our identities and thus make sense of life. In his book *The Cry for Myth*, psychologist Rollo May described myths as "the inner girders that support human personality."

Myths can be both helpful and unhelpful. The lives of real people like Mother Teresa or Gandhi or Martin Luther King, Jr. are said to have mythic proportions. They are "larger than life" and serve as models and inspiration for our own lives. Fictional heroes, like Hercules and Odysseus, offer epic stories that help us place ourselves in the journey of life.

These stories are so important to me that I have committed three years with Dr. Larry Allums, a great literature teacher who seems to know every word written in the classics, to explore these wonderful stories through a custom-designed Great Books program. I think of Larry as a "personal trainer for my mind...and my heart."

Most of us either consciously or subconsciously adopt a personal myth—a mental theme or image that informs who we are and where we belong. As our lives change, we choose from a variety of myths for inspiration and identity. But when our myth goes out of date, it can keep us stuck.

We know at some deep inner level that what made perfectly good sense several years ago is no longer a true and useful guide to life when the season changes. For example, teenage boys look to the lives of professional athletes or musicians as their own personal myths or stories. It is more than a person, more than hero worship, but imagining yourself in a situation that demands heroic behaviors. But you can't always be Michael Jordan sinking the shot that wins the game. When you hit your twenties and thirties, you are more likely to look to other sources to frame your myth.

As you approach Halftime, you are really wrestling with a changing myth. The First Half myth is the rags-to-riches Horatio Alger myth. It's the hunter-warrior slaying dragons, providing for family, establishing a commanding presence. But it is a myth that is no longer making sense after a certain point. At one time, it helped you define who you were and what you were doing. It anchored your life. But now it is confining; holding you back from becoming what you were meant to be in the *next* season of life.

"When we reach our fifties, identity becomes its own prison," wrote Keith H. Hammonds in *Fast Company*. He believes that we become so wedded to the old myth that we are blinded to even greater opportunities for a new identity. This is why it is so difficult to move from success to significance. The myth of success has been so ingrained into us that we cannot imagine anything else, least of all significance. It's right there but we don't see it.

People who are stuck between the First Half of success and a more rewarding Second Half are like the circus elephant tethered to a stake as he awaits the next show. If he wanted to, he could easily pull up the stake and go wherever he wanted. He's certainly strong enough, but he doesn't know it. He has been trained to think that that little stake will keep him confined. It's a matter of choice and habit. We choose our habits—we can choose new ones too.

Unfortunately, the danger in midlife is that we tend to make choices that actually confine us more than the First Half addiction to success. We exchange the Rags-to-Riches Myth for one that is harmful. One that keeps us from reaching the potential that the next twenty-five to thirty years promises. From my interviews and correspondence with those who have gotten stuck in Halftime, here are some of the myths that keep us staked down to an unfulfilling life:

THE PETER PAN MYTH

Nothing illustrates this myth better than the fifty-year-old who dresses (and sometimes acts) like a teenager. He still believes he can fly. That he still has it. He's in denial. He has refused to acknowledge that a season has changed and is staging an increasingly desperate attempt to relive the halcyon years of youth.

Tennessee Williams built a stellar literary career out of retelling the Peter Pan Myth (I'll be young forever): Blanche DuBois, the fading Southern belle in *A Streetcar Named Desire;* Brick, the character Paul Newman played in *Cat on a Hot Tin Roof;* Richard Burton playing the over-the-hill priest in *Night of the Iguana.*

I see this a lot in people who have been blessed with wealth. They mistakenly believe that their money can buy them eternal youth and vitality. It is this myth that has made plastic surgery a huge growth industry. There is nothing wrong with trying to look young, and I hope to always have a certain youthful mindset. But the fact is, I am not the same man I was when I was twenty-five, and in order for me to make the most out of the next twenty years, I need to leave Peter Pan behind.

When you refuse to change your myth, you deny yourself the fullness that a Second Half offers. You remain stuck in a season that increasingly becomes disheartening. You remain what you were instead of becoming what you were meant to be. The writer of Ecclesiastes reminds us that there is a season for everything. There is a time to fly and there is a time to come in for a landing.

THE LEISURE WORLD MYTH

In the previous chapter, I introduced you to a dangerous Second Half destination: Leisure World. I cannot think of a single person I know who has found the life of leisure to be what it promised: a nirvana of tension-free pleasure. And yet it is probably the universal unspoken goal of just about every man. Places like the Vintage Club in Palm Springs and whole enclaves in Aspen, Palm Beach, and Naples promise the good life. As a brief retreat, they are great. But they seldom deliver a full life if these places are your life.

I have given a lot of thought to this myth since I first wrote *Halftime*. I have seen so many people begin the Halftime journey only to get bogged down in leisure. I have come to believe that the desire for leisure—for a lifestyle unencumbered by work—is really a signal that a season has already changed. Few people in the First Half dream of quitting their jobs and playing golf all day. At least not seriously. This myth is really telling you that you are not tired of working but tired of working in your *present* capacity. Fred Smith, Sr., a retired businessman and active Christian leader, once said to me, "Work is the psychological glue that holds a man together."

In countless stories of wealthy people who do not have to work yet continue to do it, words like *mission, calling,* and *satisfaction* keep coming up. Happiness must have a goal, a challenge, something that pushes back against us.

In 1964, sociologist David Riesman wrote an essay titled "Abundance for What?" A good essay for today might be titled "Longevity for What?" One of the clearest indications that you are in Halftime is this tempting myth of full-time leisure. And one of the best ways to avoid getting stuck in midlife is to avoid falling for this myth. Take a long vacation, perhaps, but don't quit working.

THE GATSBY MYTH

This myth speaks to the need to impress, the need to maintain an illusion. It strikes often in the lives of successful people, but it is a false path to significance. F. Scott Fitzgerald's novel, *The Great Gatsby,* painted a portrait of a desperately lonely man consumed with displaying his success with the great mansion, the lavish parties, and all those custom-made shirts! All to impress Daisy Buchanan and other high-society figures. His was a quest for legitimacy and elegance with ill-gotten gain acquired from mysterious, shady enterprises on the other side of town.

The myth is "If only I had the right material symbols, the 'big people' would accept me, and I would be 'in' at last." But "in" seldom looks that pretty from the inside. Nobody came to Gatsby's funeral.

Successful people are so vulnerable to this myth, as evidenced by the advertising targeted to them. Rolex watches. Mont Blanc pens. Sleek SUVs for people who will never drive off-road. Of course there is nothing wrong with any of these products, but it is the pitch that is telling. They are positioned as products that define who you are, that separate you from the rest of the crowd. If you find yourself talking a lot about your plane, your car, your vacation home, and so on, it is probably because you and your friends are trying to gain significance in the wrong ways. These toys tend to own you, leaving you stuck in a Halftime of accumulation with the next thing sure to make you happy. It won't. You will wake up empty one day in the back of your Lear jet wondering if a G-7 would be more fulfilling.

The false promise of this myth is that once you have enough of the biggest toys, you will achieve satisfaction and fulfillment. Yet most people who get caught up in this myth never seem to have enough. When someone comes to me frustrated over being stuck in the transition from success to significance, I sometimes ask them how much time they are spending with their new toys. Things—especially big expensive things—have a tendency to own us if we are not careful. It is possible to be genuinely interested in a Second Half of greater significance but bogged down by the amount of time and energy it takes to own, maintain, and yes, enjoy so much stuff.

THE FORMER GREAT PERSON MYTH

Several years ago I had the privilege of being part of the small cadre that founded the Peter F. Drucker Foundation for Nonprofit Management and have continued as a major financial supporter throughout its life. Shortly after I sold my business, I called to speak with its director and a friend of mine, Frances Hesselbein. The reception-ist asked me over the telephone to spell my name and the nature of my business.

Former gets to be former real fast.

This is the myth that literally scares us into staying in the First Half or putting on airs in Halftime. After all, we are looking for significance. The last thing we want is to be Mr. Used-to-Be. Yet that is what we fear will happen when we phase out of our current First Half lives. So we overstay the party because we want the credit. We are no longer challenged by our work, but we hold on to the job primarily because we're afraid that if we quit, the phone will stop ringing.

I think it's important to realize that this myth, like many, has some basis in reality. If you have been a recog-nized leader in a particular field and then leave it to pur-sue something outside of that field, you will necessarily place yourself outside that circle of friends, colleagues, and business contacts. It's not that you are particularly vain and need a title or name on the door of an office. In fact, part of what is appealing about moving on is to get away from all the trappings of your corporate identity—you really *do* want to create a new environment for your truest self to emerge. And yet, our culture has promoted the myth that your identity is defined by title, business card, name on the door, or something else. Something inside tells us it is time for a new season to begin, but we hold on to the myth that our identity is wrapped up in our work.

THE HARPER LEE MYTH

Harper Lee wrote *To Kill a Mockingbird*—and not a word since. Those close to her say she was afraid to attempt another book. Her inability to live up to that "one shining moment" lead to an obscure life almost completely absent from literary circles.

Ralph Ellison is another example. He remained frozen on the trigger after the huge success of *The Invisible Man*. Forty years and not another book, though one was always in the works. His publisher has just brought out his "partially complete" work as a posthumously published novel.

Then there is the Michael Douglas character in the movie *Wonder Boys*. He plays a writer who wins the PEN award for a first novel, then retreats into academe to be the "great figure" in a writing program for admiring young students. In his ivory tower he writes page after page of worthless material. We look over his shoulder to see page 2611 in the upper right corner. He's history.

This may be the toughest myth to overcome for those of us who have been the most successful. Face it, if you've worked hard and have reached a lofty peak of success or achievement, do you really want to start all over again? That still, small voice inside is urging you to focus on something of greater and longer-lasting significance, but you know it's not going to be easy. Your "fans" who watched you build something wonderful will expect the same level of success in your next venture, and you're just not sure you can do it.

Some people never make it through Halftime because they have never recovered from their crowning achievement. They live in the past, afraid to step forward for fear of never living up to their potential. This is one of the sadder and more pathological myths in that it is built on insecurities. And yet, those who hold on to this myth stand to gain so much more by giving themselves another opportunity to succeed…only this time with significance.

THE MONEY MYTH

Soshana Zuboff is a Harvard professor who leads a special program for highly successful men and women who are at the top of their game. Once a year she convenes this Harvard Business School offering called Odyssey for thirty to forty gray-around-the-temples executives who, by their own admission, have everything yet still feel unfulfilled.

One of the questions she asks them is "How much is enough?" The answers vary, but all generally agree it's a moving target. Said one of the participants, "I used to think $1 million, but when I got there, I realized it was $10 million."

The money myth says that all you need is enough money and you can do whatever you want. It stumps Halftimers because when they start adding up the columns they conclude they don't have quite enough money to move into the Second Half. And they're right. They never will.

Money is important. Jesus talks more about money than most any other subject, and almost everything he has to say is negative. Or at least is a warning. Many times he uses the word "deceitful" when describing money. In his parable about sowing seeds, Jesus speaks of the seeds as a metaphor for spiritual life and growth. The man with seeds sown in the thorns represents those who let the "worries of this life and the deceitfulness of wealth choke it, making it unfruitful" (Matthew 13:3–23). That sounds strikingly similar to the words of *Newsweek* columnist, Robert Samuelson, who wrote, "Abundance breeds anxiety, because it gives us more freedom. We are increasingly liberated to 'be ourselves,' but self-expression can slip into self-indulgence, sometimes self-destructive."

In my late twenties, a great teacher for me was Ray Stedman, pastor of the Palo Alto Bible Church and a pioneer in the modern movement to teach Scripture. Over breakfast one morning he taught me four false beliefs that make money so deceitful. Those who have wealth have a strong tendency to believe:

- I am bulletproof (nothing can harm me)
- I am free of responsibility
- I do not need other people...or God
- Money will buy me happiness

Later in life, as I walked alone on a bluff overlooking the Rio Grande River that had taken my only son's life, I remember realizing, "You may have a lot of money, but you can't buy your way out of this." No amount of money could bring my son back. Nor can it buy any of us anything that lasts. (See chapter 6, "Adios Ross," of my book *Halftime.*)

Technology pundit George Gilder, speaking about the massive accumulation of wealth in this decade says, "Achieving prosperity without hedonism will entail heroic leadership." When we buy into the myth of money, we choke off our potential for growth and remain stuck. Only when we change myths will we be able to move on toward significance. I know many of you feel you cannot launch into a Second Half until you have just "this much more." Then you will be financially secure and can do God's work. It doesn't work that way—all the heroic stories are stories where faith comes first. Abraham left his land "even though he did not know where he was going"—*then* God provided (Hebrews 11).

THE SOLOMON MYTH

You could also call this the Renaissance Man Myth. It is the idea that if you have it all in one package—money, intelligence, and status—you will have what matters.

Solomon tried everything. Pleasure. Rational enlighten-ment. Huge building projects. One hundred wives and many more concubines. In the end, he concluded it was all vanity and chasing the wind. "Meaningless! Meaning-less! Everything is meaningless!" And what profound thought did he arrive at after trying everything: "Fear God and keep his commandments, for this is the whole duty of man." (See Ecclesiastes 12:13.)

One of the casualties of Halftime is that it can be viewed as a sort of lifelong self-improvement project. You travel. Learn a new language. Study architecture. Perfect a sport. But the focus is always on you, and ironically, that never produces fulfillment.

THE LOW COMMITMENT MYTH

People who live this myth are dabblers. They say, "I'll sit on a few boards. Do a missions trip with my church. Volunteer occasionally to help out a local non-profit." They see charity as another form of recreation, not as work. And this is socially sanctioned dabbling. People say, "That's so nice, what you are doing."

They dip in and out. Mainly these people keep themselves free for pleasure trips.

This is what Peter Drucker calls "frittering your-self away." It's a low-risk/low-return strategy, sort of like corporate bonds as an investment. You get what you put into it, which is not very much. No risk. No return. It's what chat rooms are to chat, what virtual reality is to real-ity. Close but not the real thing.

This is primarily a symptom of not really knowing "what's in the box." Frequently it is just staying busy. Hav-ing a clear and singular mission statement revolving around the "one thing" about which you are most passionate is what is needed. The Low Commitment Myth is a lot like the difference between an intramural athlete in college and a scholarship athlete. The intramural player plays a little flag football, some basketball, maybe jumps into a soccer game—has a lot of fun but realizes it's only a pastime. The scholarship athlete, on the other hand, focuses on one sport year round. It's more than a pastime; it's his reason for being at that particular college.

If your commitment is low, you are always marginal. You won't get to significance, and you're no longer in success. You become "the former success," and that's where you remain. Stuck in Halftime.

THE AGING MYTH

Despite the widespread knowledge that if you are in your forties to fifties and stand a good chance of having at least another twenty-five to thirty years of vigorous and active life ahead of you, some people buy into the myth that aging is a period of decline and decay. They hesitate to seriously step out of Halftime because they think time is running out on them. It sort of puts you in a perpetual state of regret: "I'd love to, but I'm not as young as I used to be."

The great humanitarian, Albert Schweitzer, could have said that after a distinguished career in medicine. But the first atomic explosion triggered a passion for peace that began when he turned seventy and led to his being awarded the Nobel Peace Prize in 1952. He traveled to Europe frequently to lecture until he was eighty-four and actively cared for patients in his hospital in Gabon. At eighty-seven he helped build a half-mile of road near his hospital and then designed and helped construct a bridge.

We have many other inspiring models of those who refused to accept age as an excuse for inactivity. Architect Frank Lloyd Wright began his most prolific work at the age of sixty-nine. Michelangelo was seventy-one when he was appointed chief architect of St. Peter's in Rome. Thomas Edison was still inventing in his eighties. Gandhi was sixty when he led a two-hundred mile march against the British government's salt tax.

The message I find in these examples is that age is as much a matter of predisposition as fact. It is a mindset. General Douglas MacArthur said, "Youth is not a period of time. It is a state of mind, a result of the will, a quality of the imagination, a victory of courage over timidity, of the taste of adventure over comfort." If you think of yourself as having a whole second adulthood ahead of you, you will remain at your peak. If you think time is running out, you will act like it. Better to be like Marty Greenberg, the sixty-year-old chairman of Sterling Commodities who said, "I want to stay young. I don't want to be sitting in Florida with my pants up to my chest."

It's all a matter of how you think.

These are the myths that only lead us back into Dante's "dark forest"—that keep us stuck. No wonder so many well-intentioned people fall into one or the other of these traps and never emerge again. All of these are inaccurate myths that keep us longing for the good old days of the First Half. When I moved into the Second Half by starting a parallel career, my business had been growing by 28 percent a year. From that point, the growth rate was decreased to 9 percent annually. I was tempted to believe any number of myths—from the Money Myth to the Former Great Person Myth to the Harper Lee Myth. But from my great teacher, Peter Drucker, I learned to be grateful.

"You would have given up the life you've had these last fifteen years. And for what?"

For what? That, after all, is the question we should be asking when we become tethered to First Half myths that are no longer relevant to who you are. To what end?

In the great biblical book of Exodus, the nation of Israel emerged from slavery in Egypt with a great calling from God to enter "a land flowing with milk and honey." Although they eventually made it into the land promised by God, a generation went round and round in the wilderness until they died. The great tragedy of this story is that a nation embarked on a great epic adventure assured by God that he would provide. They never were up to the challenge of leaving their biblical Halftime to the new land filled with opportunity. They lost heart.

Don't let that happen to you. Keep your dreams *ahead* of you. Opportunity is just waiting around the bend.

Section Two

INTO THE SECOND HALF

SIX

THE TWENTY-FIRST CENTURY: A WORLD OF OPPORTUNITY

The world economy is entering a long boom unlike anything ever seen before.

Peter Schwartz,
The Global Business Network

One of the foundational experiences for me in my early development was to attend what's now called the Owner-Managed Program at Harvard Business School. It's an executive education program that consists of three separate three-week sessions. I was in their second graduating class. If I were to pick a single theme that stood out for me and remained with me, it was the concept of an *"opportunity loss."* That is, not an actual loss you experience like losing money in the stock market, but a loss that derives from an opportunity that you *might* have pursued and profited from, but you didn't. It's the "road not taken" of the famous Robert Frost poem that "made all the difference."

The Second Half is a time when you can have a huge gain or loss in terms of opportunity. It's the road not taken that might have led to huge gains for the world. For me, I have set a goal of multiplying myself and my gifts a hundred fold or 100 times (I call it a season of 100X multiplication). That concept is a lot of why I do what I do.

I believe *every* single person is called to some great kingdom opportunity—an opportunity that is totally in sync with God's agenda for the world. It's the way God organized things: he gave us the opportunity to either take up the challenge or leave it be.

I believe the parable of the sower (Matthew 13) promises that each human being has the capacity to multiply "a hundred, sixty or thirty times what was sown." The variable in the parable is availability not capacity or competence. And the Parable of the Talents (Matthew 25) teaches us that God gives us opportunities in the areas in which we have skills and knowledge so that if we answer the call we will be doing exactly what he wired us to do.

This is really what the Second Half is all about: a convergence of who you really are and God's plan for mankind. You are designed to be the happiest and most content when those two themes merge into purposeful action.

For people who are followers of Christ, this might best be understood as opportunity management vs. what Dallas Willard calls "sin management." According to Willard, most Christians are more worried about sin than opportunity. They observe that nine of the Ten Commandments begin with "thou shalt not." And it *is* true that your life does not work very well if you are consumed with envy or dishonesty or adultery. All of those commandments make good sense, but you can't make a life out of what you *don't* do. It's what Taylor University president, Jay Kesler, calls "Collie Christianity"—collies don't smoke, don't drink, don't cheat on their taxes. Is that the life we want?

The goal of the Second Half is to focus more of our energy on opportunity than on sin management. In fact, opportunity is really the best form of sin management technique—to be so utterly filled and consumed with a passion for contribution to the lives of others that you just crowd out the negative parts of your life. There's a biblical parable that tells of a widow who sweeps her house clean, but then seven times as many devils come back to haunt that empty space. We can spend all our energy getting rid of sin, but if we don't replace that empty space with something better, sin will sweep back in. Nature abhors a vacuum.

In his letter to the Romans, the apostle Paul unpacks this tension between sin and opportunity where he first talks about what a wretched sinner he is; how he knows the right things to do but often does just the opposite: "I have the desire to do what is good, but I cannot carry it out" (Romans 7:18). But then he follows this agonizing over sin with that marvelous description of grace that has been made available to all of us: "Therefore, there is now no condemnation for those who are in Christ Jesus, because...the law of the Spirit of life set me free from the law of sin" (Romans 8:1).

I don't think God wired us for repression. I believe he created us to be so filled with his "Spirit of life," but we cannot live that abundant life if we focus continually on sin.

In fact, so much attention is given in Christian circles to what you can't do, that I think we need to focus on some positive commandments. I see at least twelve that are found in the Bible that could change our whole outlook about sin vs. opportunity. Grace vs. law. Here's what they instruct and where to find them:

THE TWELVE POSITIVE COMMANDMENTS

1. Love God and others (Matthew 19:19, 1 Corinthians 12, Romans 13:10)
2. Multiply and be fruitful (Genesis 1:22)
3. Trust in the Lord (Proverbs 3:5–6, Ephesians 2:8)
4. Worship God (Ecclesiastes 12:13)
5. Be available to God (Matthew 13:3–8, John 15)
6. Serve others (Matthew 25, Luke 10, James 2:14–25)
7. Find meaning through self-sacrifice (John 15:13, Romans 12:1–2, Philippians 2)
8.
9. Replace evil with good (Romans 12:21)
10. Build on strength (Romans 12, 1 Corinthians 12)
11. Pray constantly (1 Thessalonians 5:17)
12. Invest yourself (Matthew 25:14–30)
13. Forgive others (Luke 6:37)

Many Christians were brought up to focus on what they cannot do, but there's more to life than that, there's more to the Bible than that. What we need to do in the Second Half is to focus our energy on what that "more" is. Fortunately, we live in an unprecedented time where there is a lot of "more" to enjoy. Compared to the world a hundred years ago, the turn of the last century, and all of the history before then, we live in a time of tremendous opportunity blessed by three new factors:

1. LONGEVITY

In 1884, German chancellor Otto von Bismark arbitrarily set the age for retiring at sixty-five, thus inventing the Social Security pension system. It was one of those safe benefits for the government to offer, since few people lived that long. In 1900, the life expectancy for men was around forty-six years. Today, it has increased by more than *thirty* years (forty for women). Despite the fact that at age fifty you are invited to join the American Association of Retired Persons, sixty-five is awfully young to disengage.

After my son's death, I went to visit my friend and wisdom figure, Peter Drucker. Sensing that grief had overtaken me, casting a large shadow on my hopes and dreams for the future, he said to me, "Bob, you have thirty years left, and they will be the most productive thirty years of your life."

Here was a man almost thirty years my senior still publishing books and articles hugely in demand. Last year, in his ninetieth year, he was chosen by *Atlantic Monthly* magazine to write its cover article on the "information economy." Just watching Peter's productivity and his passion has had a profound effect on my thoughts about aging. Every day that Peter lives, my mental horizon extends another day. I am years down the road from that 1987 conversation with Peter, and so far he has been absolutely right.

The fact is, you *will* have more active, vigorous, and engaging years than your father did. Retirement will probably not be an option for you, not because you won't qualify at age sixty-five, but because you won't want to retire. You won't feel like it. In my second book, *Game Plan,* I urged readers to "banish retirement from your thinking." Barely four years later, I may not have to repeat that admonition because more and more "seniors" are continuing to choose to keep working. If you work things right, by the time you are sixty you will be in the middle of a Second Half career, looking for yet another opportunity to serve God and your fellowman. And when that bulge in population called the Baby Boom gets to be sixty, you can bet it is going to be very fashionable to be a young sixty.

One way to comprehend this is to look back at the past thirty years of your life. From this end, it probably seems to have rushed by, but start from the beginning and work your way forward. Look at all you have accomplished. Try to recount the highs and lows of each period (childhood, college, young adulthood, success, Halftime). When you look this way, you see that 10,950 days is a long, long time.

You have 10,000 days of vibrant living ahead of you.

2. AFFLUENCE

Despite this being a two-edged sword as you learned in the preceding two chapters, it is a documentable fact. We live in a time of unparalleled affluence, and it's not just the world of Donald Trump and Bill Gates.

According to George Will, there are 7.1 million households in the United States worth more than a million dollars (about one in fourteen and twice as many as in 1995). More than 300,000 citizens are worth ten million dollars. One of the best-selling books of the year 2000 was *The Millionaire Next Door,* which profiles this phenomenon of unprecedented affluence in America. Based on research from that book, *Money* magazine profiles the typical American millionaire: a fifty-seven-year-old male who lives in the Midwest in a house worth $320,000, drives a Ford pickup, owns and runs a small business, and is worth $3.7 million. By the year 2010, according to Kevin Kelly, the number of millionaires in America will have grown to about 20 million; 50 million in 2020. That means that in less than twenty years, the ratio of millionaires in America will be about one in three!

But even if you are not a millionaire—and I'm assuming you're not—you are far better off financially than your parents ever were, and you stand to gain even more as your 401k plans mature and you inherit your parent's property. The percentage of Americans who own stock has grown rapidly to about 45 percent of the population. If you're one of them, you ought to be paying attention to very serious market analysts who are predicting the Dow Jones Industrial Average—already on a supersonic trajectory—may zoom to 30,000 within the next four years! Maybe so. Maybe not. But times are certainly good, and odds are that it will stay that way. According to Paul Schervisch and John Havens, authors of a Boston college study on giving, aging Baby Boomers will leave behind $41 trillion to their heirs or charitable organizations.

Nope!

If you consider yourself entrenched firmly in the middle class, and all this talk of affluence seems out of reach, consider, as George Gilder has pointed out, that "the average American today lives better than the millionaires of the 1800s." Even today's poor live better than the middle class of 1950. That's because unemployment is at its lowest in two decades. Inflation hovers at 2 percent, with the economy growing at 3 percent and hourly wages up about 4 percent. As a working-class American, you are earning more money that has greater buying power in the best of economic times.

What this all means is that you really do have the financial capacity to move out of Halftime. You may not be in a position to completely quit your job, but you are indeed better off than you think. Most upper-middle-class Americans could renegotiate their work arrangements with their employers, including a decrease in salary, and have the time, energy, and money to embark on a parallel career that would provide a new center for their lives in the Second Half.

In fact, many in this socioeconomic group may benefit from the trend in the corporate world and public education of offering early retirement with lucrative contract buyouts. This might be the motivator you need to make the leap into the Second Half: freedom from your nine-to-five job, along with a significant sum of cash to get going.

3. OPTIONS

My father-in-law, like so many of his contemporaries, was an "organization man." Born in the midst of World War I and finishing high school just as the Depression gripped the United States and the world, he opted for the security of a large company. He literally spent his whole working life in one firm, the National Supply Company (now Armco Steel). As far as I know, he never seriously considered leaving the company to pursue other options, and in truth, he probably didn't have many. His company gave him a job that paid well, took care of him with a generous insurance and benefits package, and even though he is retired and in his eighties, he still benefits from that long association with a single company.

That scenario of a life locked into a single career is long gone. I don't think any college graduate believes he or she will spend a lifetime working for one company. They know that we live in a world of options.

Like our parents, we also need to learn that choice is a commodity regularly traded in today's employment environment. My hunch is that few of you who are between the ages of thirty-five and fifty-five have stayed with a single company since you began working. Most likely, you're on your third or fourth already.

And there are still plenty of choices ahead for you. Consider some of the following scenarios:

Sabbatical. Many businesses are offering their employees some form of sabbatical specifically to encourage them to engage in activities and experiences that provide a service to the community. These can be great experiments to test the water in areas that you have considered working in. Check with your company to see if they offer this option or would be interested in offering it.

Work at Home. Given your experience in the marketplace, you probably have a service or skill that someone could use. By setting up a home office and offering this service on a freelance basis, you could conceivably maintain your income needs with two to three days per week, leaving the rest of your time to invest in a Second Half opportunity.

Early Retirement. Okay, you don't like that word, but many companies are offering their senior employees (those who have been there for at least twenty years), the opportunity to "retire" early with a significant cash reward. Between your 401k, the cash, and your good health, you have the resources to move into the nonprofit sector for a smaller salary and greater significance.

You are really only limited by your creativity and willingness to risk. Most people I know who have given themselves unconventional choices have never regretted it. Most say they wish they would have done it sooner.

People who are stuck in Halftime are so focused on their present situation that they forget about these three opportunities. Think of them as A.O.L.—affluence, options, longevity. I have heard too many people say they could not move forward because they are too old or they don't have enough money or their options have narrowed. These are the ones who seem permanently stuck in midlife.

The richest messages of the Bible speak of abundance, and I believe that God intends for us to enjoy these opportunities for his kingdom's sake. The patriarch Moses left us a profound truth regarding options in Deuteronomy 30:19–20: "I have set before you life and death, blessings and curses. Now choose life, so that you and your children may live and that you may love the Lord your God, listen to his voice, and hold fast to him." Jesus said that he came into this world so that we would have life and "have it to the full."

A life limited by our own choices is a tragic life that will never become what God fully intended. We were created to make a difference, to leave something behind of meaning. At no time in history have we had such opportunity to enjoy life to its fullest in ways that bring happiness and fulfillment to ourselves, and betterment for those who need it.

SEVEN

NEW RULES FOR THE SECOND HALF

*In times of drastic change, it is the learners who
inherit the future. The learned find themselves
equipped to live in a world that no longer exists.*
Eric Hoffer

The best way to get out of Halftime and on your
way into a Second Half of significance is to realize that all
the rules have changed. Life is no longer what it used to
be when you started out twenty or thirty years ago. Consider some of the changes that have happened in that brief
time period:

> You did not own a computer or use one when you first
> started working
>
> Email was nonexistent
>
> Many of you still had rotary phones in your offices—
> none of you had cell phones or voice mail
>
> Using an express-mail service such as FedEx was an
> unusual and much-to-be avoided expense
>
> Copiers printed in gray and white
>
> You used overhead projectors in your presentations

Congregations of large churches were measured in the several hundreds rather than the thousands

Luxury homes hovered around $100,000

There was no such thing as an IRA

Microwaves cost $1,000 and were the size of a small stove

Only banks sold CDs—you played your music on vinyl or eight-track

The word "dotcom" meant nothing to anyone

Communism was a dominant world force

Just about everything that defined your world twenty-five years ago has changed, and along with the new world comes new rules. For example, if you wanted to start a new business in the seventies, you started meeting with bankers and searched for a building and began looking for partners. Today, you register your domain name on the Internet and have at it with your dotcom.

SO WHAT ARE THE NEW RULES?

Begin with yourself. In the last chapter we looked at the myriad opportunities awaiting you, compared to the world in which your parents grew up. In the First Half, you sent your résumé out and hoped to get a bite. You began with whatever opportunity came along.

In the Second Half, you must begin with yourself. The opportunities for you now are so overwhelming and multiple that you have to start with your own unique abilities, calling, history, and giftedness before you can even look at the opportunities.

You are responsible for choosing the right opportunity, and to do that you must be reintroduced to yourself. Just as the times have changed, you and your circumstances have also changed. As Peter Drucker has written in the foreword to this book, the most important event in our age is that for the first time in the history of the world, we will have to learn how to "manage ourselves." Where the First Half emphasis has been on fitting yourself to the needs of an organization, in the Second Half you will need to know more about yourself than ever. You are probably worth more. Your children may be on their own or close to it. Some of your values may have changed.

The best way to get at this is to simply ask yourself some questions and answer them honestly. Questions like: What do I believe? What am I most passionate about? What would I really like to be doing if I could? What would challenge me more than anything I've ever done before? What has my whole life up to now prepared me to do?

There are several formal inventories and methods for doing this as well. Halftime, which I founded two years ago to help people move from success to significance (see *www.Halftime.org*), uses a tool called G.R.A.S.P. which leads business and professional people through a process to discover their

> G rounding
> R oles
> A bilities
> S piritual gifts
> P assions

The Willow Creek Association, founded by Willow Creek Community Church in Barrington, Illinois, has developed an entire curriculum called Network that can also help you get a clearer picture of what makes up the unique "you."

And, of course, there's the classic work that Dick Bolles has literally devoted his life to: *What Color Is Your Parachute?* It is updated every year and has an excellent section on callings and your mission in life.

And now there's a wonderful new video curriculum for small groups based on my first book, *Halftime.* A film crew traveled all over the country to find great Halftime stories that help you work through the various issues you will face in your journey from success to significance. I've always recommended that you should never attempt a Halftime experience on your own, and this new tool is designed to help you process your Halftime experience with a group of fellow travelers (see *www.halftime.org*). The transition to a focus on significance seems to work best when it has three characteristics: it happens locally, over time, with others.

The important thing to realize is that before you can move forward out of Halftime, you need to get a handle on who you are. Everything starts there if you want to make the journey successfully and with as few false starts as possible.

Take care of your family first. Family is a major Halftime concern in the stories I hear. People can see the "empty nest" coming and don't want their kids to grow up without knowing their moms and dads. Frequently, the marriage itself needs more attention. Doing it gradually, not suddenly ("Honey, I'm home!") usually works better. Halftime is often a quest for rebalancing if not reporting. People too consumed with work want to reallocate more time to their family. More flexibility. Less travel time. Just say no. If you're not able to say no in business, you're dead. Even more so in Halftime.

Find an organizational vehicle that fits your dream. I am a big fan of the nonprofit organization as a

tremendous opportunity for Second Half service. According to Peter Drucker in his book, *Managing the Non-
Profit Organization,* nonprofits are America's largest
"employer." He cites the fact that one of every two American adults serves as a volunteer in the nonprofit sector
and spends at least three hours a week in nonprofit work.

Too many times, people feel the need to do something significant as they approach Halftime but basically
expend a lot of time, energy, and resources reinventing
something that a nonprofit is already doing (and doing
better). Before you embark on your own venture, check
to see if there is a nonprofit organization that matches
your interests. I can assure you that they need your
knowledge, experience, and skill sets.

Build on the islands of health and strength. Find
a 100X organization with a 100X leader and help them
turbo charge. Better to find an organization that needs
high-test skills to move a growth agenda forward.

In many ways, this is counterintuitive for many
people in Halftime because they tend to look for the need-
iest cause and kind of form a victim/rescuer relationship.
Or they answer the first call for help. That may be just perfect for some individuals, but what I've found is that the
former executive who thinks his Second Half mission is
to volunteer at a soup kitchen usually tires of it and goes
back to being stuck in Halftime.

I know that sounds harsh, but I think experience
bears it out as true. It goes back to fully understanding
yourself and being a good steward of what God has given
you. That is why I use the term "100X" to help me focus
on what I ought to be doing. I want the highest possible
return on my investments of time and money for the kingdom of God. The case could be made that if you have the
entrepreneurial skills to start and run a growing business,

you could be more effective starting a new organization that looks after a hundred soup kitchens, thus multiplying your impact to thousands of recipients of those services.

That doesn't mean you isolate yourself from real problems. The best hospital administrators admit themselves to their hospitals on a regular basis so that they fully understand how the patient views the care and treatment they receive. If your mission is to provide entrepreneurial support for soup kitchens, you also *should* volunteer to ladle out soup to the homeless on a regular basis. But you will probably be better at raising capital than ladling soup.

A key biblical story that illustrates this new rule for the Second Half is where Jesus had five thousand hungry people to feed and just five loaves of bread and two fish. The Bible says he took what he had and blessed it and through some incredibly miraculous happening, there was enough to feed the five thousand with plenty left over. And I really believe that's how God's kingdom is. That with me alone it is five loaves and two fishes, but with God I will have enough to feed five thousand.

Just do it! Jacob Bronowski wrote in *The Ascent of Man* that "the world can only be grasped by action, not by contemplation."

Too many people are stuck in Halftime after several years because they are overthinking the problem. They want the perfect plan before they embark. At some point you have to jump in, even if everything isn't in place. It may never be. The Second Half is not about perfection but effectiveness. The new reality in the business world is that you have to be agile; ready to change directions. You can't afford to wait until you have everything in place because the velocity of business is so rapid. It's not just the business world. You may need to embark and figure it out along the way.

There's biblical precedent for this idea. The great Bible teacher Ray Stedman once told me about a story from the Old Testament where a prophet embarks on the road and the voice of God comes up from *behind* him—not before him—to tell him he's heading the right direction. I think a lot of people in Halftime need to say, "Even in the face of imperfect evidence, I'm going to embark on this road and let the voice of God come up behind me and tell me if I'm on the right or wrong road." Follow your dream. Let the experience itself teach you what to change. As Henry Blackaby says, "Find where God seems to be at work and help out." The poet Muchado said, "We make the path by walking."

Work only with the receptive. After Jesus chose the twelve men who would help him start a movement that continues to this day, he sent them out on a mission. He didn't give them much of a plan or any financing (see previous rule). Just go out two by two from village to village, he said, and live off the kindness of those willing to help you. If a village wasn't receptive to what they were trying to do, they were to "shake the dust off your feet" and move on to the next village.

Throughout the First Half you've had to work with people who weren't always on the same page as you. Part of what motivated you, but also drained your energy and resources, was selling your point of view to those who were not as enthusiastic as you. In the Second Half, you need to work with those individuals and organizations whose dream is aligned with your dream.

I have found that once word gets out that you're looking for a meaningful mission for your Second Half, you need to be very selective. There will be no shortage of organizations that will approach you for help. You can spend the rest of your life wasting a lot of energy and resources with people who don't share your passions and values. You only have so much time and sooner or later you will find a group of people who are dying to do what you want to do. Trust me. It's there.

Pay your dues. Bill Donaldson is an extraordinary man I met through the Young Presidents Organization (YPO). Donaldson has had careers in business, academe, and government. He started out as an investment banker, (he was the "D" in DLJ), then moved into the political arena, working for people like Hugh Carey, the former governor of New York and former secretary of state Henry Kissinger. When I met him he was the dean of the Yale School of Management, and after that he became president of the New York Stock Exchange. He says it is very difficult to traverse all three sectors because the rules are different in each one. In business, the rules are the bottom line. In government, it's "who's got the power?" In the academic world, it's all about process.

If you are going to change fields in your Second Half, you will have to pay your dues and learn the rhythm and rules of a new sector. You cannot operate in one arena as you did in another. Many First Half business types think they would like to move into a nonprofit ministry, higher education, or politics. More than one business executive has shared his dreams with me of being the executive pastor at a large church or the president of a college. Often, they get stalled because they haven't learned the rules of these games. They did not have enough experience in their new game to be effective. Switching fields requires that you spend a good amount of time listening rather than coming in as the "instant expert." You can change your game, but you can't change the rules of that game. That takes years, sometimes decades, to do. I know this from my work in the church world.

All work is done in teams. First Halfers are fighter pilots. They have a bit of renegade in them—rugged individualists in the best sense of the American pioneer spirit. You probably would not be where you are today if you had not pushed pretty hard on the throttle.

In the Second Half, one of your most important objectives is to build your dream team. The best contributions you will make will be the result of working in teams. I don't start any new enterprise without first forming a team of like-minded individuals who will help me turn a dream into a reality. Peter Drucker is fond of saying that if you crossed John McEnroe with Albert Einstein, you might come out with the mental acuity of John McEnroe with the manual dexterity of Albert Einstein.

The reason this is so important is that your Second Half mission will be the biggest mission of your life—much bigger than anything you've ever done in your present career. You can't afford to go it alone.

Building a team can be anything from running your ideas past a small group of trusted friends to actually inviting a few selected people to join you in your Second Half venture. Whatever you do, if you are married, make sure your spouse is on your team. In a healthy marriage, spouses can offer the best insights into Second Half ventures. They know you better than any other teammate and will help keep you appropriately grounded.

Find a mentor. Tom Tierney told me he would rather have ten hours with one influential individual mentor than twenty hours with a team. For most of us having someone who knows us well enough, who is farther down the same road we are now seeking to travel, and who *cares* is the "pearl of great price." And more often it's the missing element when you are attempting a break-though. That has certainly been the case for me. If you look closely at your circle of friends and acquaintances, you will find two or three people who are ten to twenty years your senior and would love to be a sounding board for your ideas. And when they speak, listen!

These are just some of the ways you will need to play the game differently in the Second Half. There are others, like *reallocate yourself to a new identity* (you're not the CEO anymore), *run with the unexpected success* (instead of trying to figure out why it worked or allocating yourself to hopeless causes), and *invest in people more than profit* (let the First Halfers build the economy), but I think you get the idea. It's a whole new ball game with a new set of rules.

If you find yourself stuck in Halftime, maybe you need to look at the rules that you're playing by. One of the biggest mistakes I see people make who are sincere about a Second Half career but are floundering in Halftime is that they are doing everything "business as usual."

Stop now and ask yourself: What has changed? What are the new rules of *my* Second Half?

If you wanted business as usual, you would still be in the First Half.

EIGHT
THE HALFTIME
TRANSITION TOOLBOX

*The ordinary arts we practice every day at home
are of more importance to the soul than their
simplicity might suggest.*

Thomas Moore

Consider this chapter a "refresher course" that will
help you get unstuck. It will deal with a lot of the practical matters that are necessary for a successful transition.
If you have read *Halftime* or *Game Plan,* it may have a
familiar ring to it. Treat it like a toolbox. You can't use
every tool at the same time. Reach for the tool that seems
to fit the situation you are involved with as you take steps
toward your Second Half journey.

MONEY

One of the most frequent questions I get about the
Second Half is "How much money will I need?" When the
famous union boss, John L. Lewis, was asked how much
was enough, he answered, "More." And unfortunately,
most people in Halftime think that's the right answer and
thus never get into the Second Half.

The answer I like to give to that question sounds flippant: "Just enough." But in all honesty, I cannot think of a single individual in the Second Half who has run out of money, and there are a lot of upper-middle-class people on that journey. If God is in it, I can assure you that you will have enough money. Money should never stand in the way of your doing something significant with the Second Half of your life. One of the reasons you're ready to leave the First Half is because it has focused so much on getting and spending money.

Still, you will need money in your Second Half—either money you have already earned and invested, or a source of money to provide for your needs as well as finance your mission. That will vary from person to person, but you should not think about the Second Half without thinking about money. My assumption is that you will not be able to simply quit your job and not have to be concerned about money. You will need some regular source of income to maintain an acceptable standard of living while fully engaged in a Second Half career that is fulfilling. So let's first look at some options for those of you who will need to continue creating income while you are engaged in your Second Half mission:

Low-Cost Probes. Instead of jumping into a season of life, make some careful forays into areas of interest that could develop into your Second Half mission. For example, let's say you are interested in doing something for inner-city youth. Your ultimate goal might be to purchase an old building, turn it into a youth center, and begin offering a variety of services to help young people prepare for college. Before you take out a second mortgage on your house, volunteer with an existing youth program to gain some experience and perspective. It will not only confirm whether or not this is really what you want to do, but it will plug you into a network of contacts that will be helpful should you eventually decide to take the plunge. In the meantime, you will not be draining a lot of cash from your bank account. It's an affordable way to take some positive steps toward your Second Half goals.

Parallel Career. This is probably the best way for a person dependent on an income to successfully move into the Second Half. A parallel career is really a gentle plan for holding two jobs. It often involves renegotiating your working relationship with your employer so that you have blocks of time to invest in your Second Half career.

The parallel career option is especially compatible with the professions (law, education, medicine, etc.) where employees have some autonomy in determining their workload. An attorney, for example, can arrange to carry fewer clients (at a commensurate reduction in income) so that she can devote one or two days a week to a Second Half initiative. Public school teachers could conceivably use their summers to launch a Second Half career that eventually could supplant their teaching income, thus serving as a very convenient transition out of Halftime.

I am convinced that the parallel career concept could help most of the people who feel as if they are stalled in Halftime. It's really a win-win: You get to keep your job, which means you will still have your identity as well as a source of income. If your Second Half endeavor doesn't work out, you won't be out in the cold and will have the resources to try something else. And most employers would much rather keep a valued employee on a part-time basis rather than having to recruit and train a brand new employee.

More with Less. Another option for people who want a Second Half career yet depend on a regular salary is to develop a downward mobility plan. This is just another way of answering the question "How much is enough?" There's a certain leveling off that occurs in midlife that allows people to live for less than they did during the child-rearing home-furnishing years. It is not by chance that the Second Half and the "empty nest" approach at roughly the same time. You have more time available and you need less money. And there are some concrete things you can do to lower your expenses even more. A smaller house could give you up to an additional $500 a month in savings/income. Do you really need that boat, or could you rent one the two weeks out of the year you use it? Do you really enjoy belonging to those clubs or are you doing it because of certain expectations.

Newspaper columnist Scott Burns recently observed that it's not so much the amount of money we have that determines our financial health, but how we manage what we have. To that end, he began a contest for his readers, inviting them to submit ideas for better money management. One reader wrote how he tries to calculate the "actual" price of any new purchase, based on what would happen if he invested that money instead. So when he got the urge to buy a large screen television for $1,500, he considered the return on that $1,500 if he invested it for ten years at a modest 8 percent: $1,829.46. Thus, the actual price for the television was really $3,329.46.

That may seem a bit extreme, but it helps illustrate how being a little more frugal can pay off in real dollars. Remember the warnings about leisure and material possessions. Neither live up to their promises and are usually a tremendous drain on your finances.

While I believe the majority of those who seek a more significant Second Half will need to remain employed, there are a growing number of people who will have access to larger sums of money. People who like me have been able to sell a business, but also the beneficiaries of our current booming economy who have watched their once modest stock holdings turn into literally small fortunes. The danger is to think you can do just about anything you want, with little regard for money when the fact is you simply have more to lose if you are not careful.

My basic principle here is to set aside an amount that guarantees financial security for your family. Or if your family has left the nest, calculate the amount you and your spouse will need to maintain the lifestyle you decide is appropriate plus some for a margin of safety. Then allocate the rest to significant purposes without the slightest fear of insolvency. When I sold my business, I, with the help of my financial planner, put together a plan that will allow my wife, Linda, and me to continue living well and still give away most of what we own in our lifetimes and the rest (hopefully not much) when we die. As far as I am concerned—may the last check bounce! Why pass the burden on to someone else? It's your calling, not theirs. God calls individuals, not organizations—not even families.

I also recommend you keep short accounts with your spouse on all of your Second Half plans, but especially as it relates to money. Nothing gets you bogged down in Halftime like arguments with your spouse over your desire to give away something that belongs to both of you. If you are not on the same page about this, you will never make it into the Second Half.

Finally, you really need to examine your own attitudes about money. Most wealthy people simply can't deal with the idea of not having their wealth line moving in any direction other than upwards and to the right. A big question you will have to answer here is whether you want to practice charity or accumulation. The Bible talks about the addiction to material things as a form of idolatry where your possessions become your master instead of your servant. God's joke on rich people is that they will have to leave it *all* behind. It's better and more responsible to allocate it yourself while you have the energy to do so. That's what I am doing.

TIME

If you believe the adage "Time is money" (which I do), then you will need to be just as careful about how you manage time as to how you manage money. It is a limited resource—much more limited than money—and if you are not careful, you will squander it to the point that you are not effectively contributing to your Second Half goals.

Pacing is a big issue for people in Halftime, especially for those who are not dependent on a regular salary. Initially, you feel as if you have all this time on your hands and become careless about managing it. If you try to do too much too fast, you will burn out. If you give in to the temptation to spend too much time on your leisure pursuits, you will rust out. It's a delicate balancing act that many new Halftimers report as being a struggle.

The best solution I have found comes from the Strategic Coach program developed by Dan Sullivan. The idea is to divide your complete calendar into three types of days: focus days, buffer days, free days.

Focus days. These are when you are focused on producing the specific outcomes that are the living out of your commitments. These are performance days. Like a baseball player or a ballerina, this is when the crowd is assembled and you are onstage.

Buffer days. These are days when you are getting ready for focus days. You are preparing. You are making clear (you hope) work assignments to other team members. You are hearing reports and taking corrective action to clean up all the messes you thought would be successes. You are returning calls, keeping commitments, developing relationships.

Free days. Free days are for rejuvenation for doing all the things outside your business that bring balance to your life and renew your energy. Most of us "work tired" most of the time. We never get fresh and focused. We never get creative, and worst of all, we lose touch with God (recall Ken Blanchard's E.G.O. concept, mentioned in chapter 3) and allow our closest relationships to fray for simple lack of attention—we're "there" but we're not *really* there for those we love most. A free day is a twenty-four-hour period, midnight one day to midnight the next, completely free from work-related problem solving, communication, and action. The Strategic Coach program teaches that taking time off is not a luxury but a necessity for successful entrepreneurs who want to be at their creative, focused best.

When you're focused, you're intense, sharp, on point. When you're free, you are *totally* free. Rest and regeneration is the point and it's the *only* point. For me these are my creative days. I lessen the din of focus and buffer days. I watch movies. I get human again. I make time to be once again fascinated with my wife. I am released from the compulsion to stay on schedule. Very seldom does something come up that won't queue up for attention on a focus day or a buffer day. The Bible calls this a Sabbath. Even God rested after he created the world. Try it. You have permission. It's in the Bible!

And don't worry about being less productive. I know one entrepreneur, a financial planner, who uses this system and who went so far as to "delegate" the bottom 80 percent of his client list to his competitors in order to focus exclusively on his best customers and to have free days with his family. His business went up—dramatically!—and he had free days for the first time in his life. Try it! It will keep you sane and in the game for a long run. You will be less likely to get tired and make a big error, perhaps *the* big error that we all worry about. (Dan Sullivan's excellent tape and booklet titled *The Time Breakthrough* can be obtained at *www.strategiccoach.com.*)

WHAT'S IN THE BOX?

In *Halftime* I described how I hired a strategic planner to help me decide what to do with the rest of my life. After spending several hours interviewing me, he concluded that before he could help me I had to sort out my loyalty to two allegiances: my faith and my money. He asked me to put only one inside a box, and once I did that he could tell me how to design my Second Half. It was probably the best exercise I have ever conducted in terms of giving me clarity about my Second Half.

If you are stuck in Halftime, you may need to go back and repeat that exercise. I have found several people who thought they had put the right thing in the box, only to discover they still were trying to cram two or three things into that position of priority. It won't work. In my case, I've updated "the box." It used to be a cross, symbolizing my faith in Christ, but I've focused it now to 100X, which is the message I receive from the Parable of the Talents and the Parable of the Sower. 100X has come to symbolize my new objective in expressing my faith in action and service. Peter Drucker says you should be able to get your personal mission on the front of a T-shirt. "100X" is what is on my T-shirt. What's on yours?

Many people put "God" in their boxes but find he is too big to handle. It's kind of like the little boy in Sunday school who was asked by his teacher pointing to a picture of a squirrel, "What's this?" The boy replied, "It looks like a squirrel to me, but I'll bet the answer is Jesus." People of faith are so conditioned to give the right answer (obviously God is to be the center of their lives) that they may not have wrestled enough with the question "What's *really* in the box for me personally?" And if the answer truly is God, try to break it down into a brief action statement. The apostle Paul talks of working out your salvation, and I don't think he meant we are saved by the work we do for God. Rather, he is reminding us that faith without action just sort of hangs out there and is meaningless. Pretty soon it atrophies like the unused muscle of a hospital patient—all healing and no regeneration. Worse still, faith without expression grows cynical. So instead of putting God or Jesus in the box, think of how you would like to work out your salvation.

SELF-ASSESSMENT

If you have read *Halftime* or *Game Plan,* you know that I am a huge proponent of self-assessment. Peter Drucker says that most professional people do not know who they are. He says that we tend to downplay our strengths (we take them for granted) and that we surely do not know our weaknesses. For that reason, many people head into the Second Half attempting things for which they have little or no competency or interest. Frequently we are reacting to what I call OPA (other people's agenda) rather than defining what we do best, what God is calling *us* to do.

One of the biggest mistakes I see among Christians is to automatically assume your Second Half must be something that falls into the category of church work. I don't know how many men have told me they wanted to become pastors. This is why I like to use the term, kingdom work, because in my mind that broadens the possibilities immensely. For example, Don Williams is chairman of the board of one of the nation's top real estate firms, the Trammell Crow Companies. When he began asking himself Halftime questions, he was wise enough to look for a Second Half career that would use his strengths in negotiating complex relationships. Don was in literally thousands of partnerships in his First Half. Recently he renegotiated his relationship with Trammell Crow so that he could develop a parallel career (still one of the best ways to enter the Second Half). And what is he doing? He's engaged in a very ambitious project to rehabilitate the troubled southern sector of Dallas. He's using the skills and competencies that he developed at Trammell Crow to transition into a Second Half life of fulfillment and significance. He's making a difference for thousands of people, and he is living out a dream he had for years.

Jack Willome, who was president of the largest home builder in San Antonio, took two years off for self-assessment (not completely, but mostly) after selling his company. Jack says, "I feel like God gave me the financial ability to buy my time back." He frequently cautions others to take time to "recover" from business. Now he helps a small group of nonprofit enterprises achieve clarity about mission and focus. My Leadership Network is one of them, and his contribution will be a critical factor in our continued success. (For an excellent audiotape of Jack's transition story, see *www.halftime.org*).

As far as the tool you use for self-assessment, I don't think it really matters. Sometimes the best self-assessment is just asking yourself some key questions: What am I good at? What do I like doing? Am I a people person, or am I more comfortable working in an analytical mode? What was my proudest moment in my work? What do I care about, really? I have found that busy people seldom take the time to work through these questions, so that may be the first step for you.

But I would also recommend a more formal type of tool to help you get at the very core of who you are and what you are most suited to do. Every bookstore is crowded with them in the self-improvement section, and all of them achieve the same purpose: to get you to sit still long enough to look at yourself objectively. I packed a lot of them into *Game Plan,* but you will also find them in many other works. Peter Drucker has just produced an excellent interactive CD-ROM tool on "Managing Oneself." It is available from *www.corpedia.com.*

The point here is not to simply rely on hunches but to do some spadework in determining your skills and knowledge as well as your personality. It will save you a lot of false starts if you have a clear picture of what you are best suited to do.

A BRAND NEW BHAG

Jim Collins, the brilliant coauthor of *Built to Last,* found in his studies that long-lasting companies have what he called a BHAG: a Big Hairy Audacious Goal—a problem so large that it could not be solved in one corporate leader's tenure, something that drew them forward into the future.

Probably the biggest problem keeping so many people stuck in Halftime is a failure of the imagination to dream big enough, to see far enough forward. The Second Half is more than volunteering occasionally for a nonprofit or taking a missions trip. Think of what attracted you to your First Half career: challenge, excitement, risk. I believe God has wired us in such a way that we are at our best when we set our sights on things beyond our reach. It is the spirit that gave us the Thomas Edisons, the Henry Fords, the Mother Teresas. To be successful in moving out of Halftime, you need to tap into that same spirit. I once heard Philadelphia insurance company founder Arthur DeMoss describe his Second Half this way, "I want to attempt something so impossible that unless God is in it, it is doomed to failure."

Robert Lewis has been a successful pastor in Little Rock, Arkansas, who recently found himself in Halftime. He had led his church to tremendous growth, not just numerically but spiritually as well. His people love him and he could easily stay there preaching and teaching until he retires. But he sensed he had gone about as far as he should go with this leg of his church's journey, and he sensed that inner need to do something different.

Many pastors in this situation either look for another church and start all over or start a brand new church. But Robert had a BHAG, what might be called a Big *Holy* Audacious Goal—a dream so big that most people think it's impossible. He has started an organization called I Squared (I^2), which stands for squaring the influence of his church. He plans to plant a hundred churches in Arkansas, influence a thousand different churches across the United States by consulting, and touch ten thousand pastors in terms of improving their competency over the next fifteen years!

That's the type of goal you have to have in mind in Halftime or you'll only dabble in the Second Half. An ironic twist to the Robert Lewis story above: He knew he needed some high-powered help to accomplish this goal, so he set out to recruit executives from the business community. Today he has attracted top quality business leaders who have involved themselves in Robert's dream. They wouldn't have gotten involved if the dream was small and reachable. It was the BHAG nature of the project that attracted them.

So if you're stuck, take a second or third look at your dream. Is it big enough? Is it stated in measurable terms that seem impossible to reach? It's one thing to say you want to change America. But to say you're going to influence ten thousand pastors is both measurable and a little bit crazy as well. Knowing Robert, he will probably get it done. But say he only influences five thousand pastors? Pretty great!

THE OPPORTUNITY SCAN

Once you are clear about the focus of your Second Half career, you need to be very deliberate about observing the environment in terms of kingdom needs. As I mentioned above, do not limit yourself to church work, though some will end up working with or for a church or parachurch organization. For example, John DiIulio one of America's leading sociologists, has moved from Princeton where he was the youngest-ever tenured faculty member to the University of Pennsylvania in order to head a massive research project that will prove emphatically what most of us sense—that faith-based organizations get better results than others (twice the result for half the cost is what I suspect). I'm contributing to his work because I believe it seems to be what God is doing now: fashioning some new equation of public/private, religious/secular partnerships to work on the most intractable issues in America's inner cities. John's findings may shape public policy for years to come. Churches are a critical part but they aren't the whole picture.

I do not want for a minute to imply that you should not include the church in your opportunity scan. But the kingdom of God is so much bigger than the church, and one of the real growth opportunities you ought to include in your search is the private social sector. According to *The Economist*, "charity is being asked to do more, as government tries. . .to do less." Former CEO and chairman of Citicorp, Walter Wriston, predicts that the fastest-growing business in the next twenty years will be the administration of private foundations. He bases that prediction on the fact that our prosperous economy will produce a huge pool of talented executives who would rather be engaged in something more productive than playing golf. (See *Wired* magazine, September 1999.)

The key issue here is to look widely and far enough to find opportunities that match up to your "one thing" and that could become a vehicle for chasing down your own BHAG.

STRATEGIC PLANNING

Just as soon as I say something about planning, I can hear some of you reminding me that in the last chapter I encouraged you to "Just do it!" without thinking too much about it. A little schizophrenia here? Not really. The key is balance. Obviously, you could spend the rest of your life fine-tuning the perfect plan for the Second Half of your life, only to realize the Second Half is drawing to a close. Rather, part of your Halftime interlude should be given over to some deliberate thinking of who you are, what you want to do, and how you're going to do it.

A strategic plan can be as simple as a few pieces of legal pad on which you draw a plan for getting from where you are now to where you want to be. It is not something you should attempt in a few hours, but a process stretching over a period of time. I also recommend you involve others (see "Build a Halftime Team" below), and most certainly your spouse.

Try this: find a physical space that relaxes you most. Close your eyes and let your imagination roam by prompting your mind to: "Make a picture of your life as it would be if it were perfect." Visualize where you would be, what you would be doing, and who you would be doing it with. Say: "This is my most ideal day—the perfect day of my dreams." Sometimes your visual imagination can develop a richer, more profound picture for you than using your rational faculties alone. A mental image can give you a picture that is too complex to be expressed in words alone combining your history, your passions, and "the still, small voice of God as well." I have drawn in my journal a pretty full picture that includes the major elements in my life—all on one page. Try it and see what happens for you.

One of the best ways to take stock of your past, present, and future is a method called the Stage 10 Dream that comes from The Strategic Coach, the program for entrepreneurs. Basically, it suggests you divide your life from birth to present into five stages and try to describe the character of each of those periods. What was the nature of your work, your income, your significant relationships, your accomplishments. Then, you select a year that represents what you forecast to be the end of your active life and work back to the present dividing those years into five segments. For example, I divided my first sixty years into the five segments that seem to hang together. For me the stages were

Stage 1—Early individual achievement
Stage 2—Learning to lead and manage
Stage 3—Super growth of the company
Stage 4—Parallel career
Stage 5—Selling the company to pursue my 100X dream

Then I selected age seventy-five as Stage 10—a time when I expect I will begin to have less energy and divided the next fifteen years into five three-year segments, which I try to visualize for a "dream Second Half."

The "look back" is a way of recapping your history in a very positive way because most people don't realize how positive their lives have been. The look ahead is to try and determine what you want Stage 10 to look like—what your fully realized dream of a life well lived would be. What this exercise does is help you identify how you want to make a lasting contribution based on the qualities and skill sets that brought you to your present situation and to get highly concrete about Stage 6, the next stage in your journey (for me it's the next three years). Here's another question from The Strategic Coach seminar:

> If we were meeting here three years from today–and you were to look back over those three years to today, what has to have happened during that period both personally and professionally for you to feel happy about your progress?

BUILD A HALFTIME TEAM

I do not think I have attempted anything that amounted to much without seeking help from others. And

I do not think you can successfully get out of Halftime without assembling a team to offer new perspectives, to hold you accountable, and to provide encouragement to and fill out needed competencies. You begin with an assessment of your own special abilities, and, as Peter Drucker reminds us in the foreword to this book, they are easy to miss. Because they are the things that come naturally to you, you take them for granted. These are the engaging occupations where you completely lose track of time when you are doing them. Unfortunately, the rugged individualism that served us so well in the First Half prevents many in Halftime from seeking help from others. We need others to fill in our blind spots. We're not "whole" without them.

My approach to boards is highly pragmatic. For example, there are times when I convene a "once only" board of directors—a few trusted friends whom I will invite to spend part of a day with me so I can bounce some ideas off them. My friend, Don Williams, calls this a "sanity check." I also have a regularly convened board of directors who assume a more active continuing interest in the operation of my Second Half enterprise, Leadership Network, a board for Halftime, and an advisory board for the Buford Foundation, which looks over all that I do, both personally and as a social entrepreneur including all of the finances. No secrets.

I also put together a list, representing the top twenty relationships that will be the most productive in terms of significance. These are people who will be most likely to contribute something useful within the next ninety days. They are the ones I rely on for help with the projects I am focused on right now.

Then I have my "Farm Club," twenty individuals with whom I have established a close relationship but who I most likely will not contact as frequently. These two groups give me a huge resource of talented people who I am partnering with in some fashion during my Second Half.

One important consideration: You cannot manufacture relationships. To develop a relationship you have to invest in it. It could be that you have tried to build a team of people with whom your relationship is mostly superficial. You cannot possibly expect to receive much from a team like that. Even if your list of potential teammates is small, it is best to include only those with whom you have earned the right to approach for assistance.

FIND YOUR ROLE

I believe one of the unintentional effects of my first book, *Halftime,* is that it left the impression that there is a single role for you to play in the Second Half, and that role is one of leader or entrepreneur. Therefore, some may be stuck in Halftime because they may never be able to fit that role.

Actually, I see at least five roles that are legitimate avenues to significance in the Second Half. Each goes beyond the roles of small donor and occasional volunteer. None is more important than the other, and where you fit in has a lot to do with what you have discovered in your self-assessment.

The Hero. This is the top gun; the one who assumes leadership. A true entrepreneur who enjoys risk and has the qualities of a leader—the ability to develop a BHAG and recruit talented people and money to convert the dream to reality.

The Hero's Partner. Fans of the magazine *Christianity Today* know that Harold Myra is the publisher and is seen as the visionary leader who built the magazine into a family of eight successful publications. What some do not always realize is that Paul Robbins has been alongside providing much of the business support for the enterprise. Harold is the hero; Paul the hero's partner. You may fit best as a partner, working alongside someone more comfortable being out front. I have been Frances Hesselbein's partner in the first ten years of the Peter F. Drucker Foundation for Nonprofit Management. I feel that I have made an important and valuable contribution in that role.

The Hero's Patron. People with a true gift for making money ought to consider the role of patron as Second Half career. But here I am not talking about a disinterested donor who merely writes checks, but an active partner in the enterprise so that he or she assumes "ownership." The great story of patronage is the Medici family who sponsored the Renaissance in art in fifteenth-century Florence. The patrons were as central to this golden age as were the artists. No patrons. No great art.

The Hero's Expert. Here again, it may be that the role you will play best is in providing guidance to someone who has formed a Second Half enterprise. Ken Jennings, an exAir Force fighter pilot and instructor, has left a seven-figure annual income partners slot at Anderson Consulting to begin VentureWorks, a firm that seeks to bring Anderson level consulting to bear on Christian enterprises. Tom Tierney, the worldwide chairman of Bain & Company, has just (Spring 2000) announced the formation of the Bridge Group to bring the sort of world-class expertise to bear on social sector organizations that giant corporations have received for years. Why shouldn't nonprofit work get the first team? Man doesn't live by bread alone.

The Hero's Team. Quite a few people who have more money than meaning in their lives are switching to full-time work in nonprofit organizations. They join the staff on a paid basis to play a forty-hour-a-week role on the leadership team of an organization that connects with their passions. The pay is less but they find the focus on doing something that makes a difference in peoples' lives well worth the economic sacrifice.

John Purcell, who honed his corporate skills at Westinghouse is now executive pastor at Perimeter Church in Atlanta, where over nine thousand people attend each week in fifteen locations. Gary Schwammlein, who headed international operations for the NutraSweet division of Monsanto, is now heading international development for the Willow Creek Association based in Chicago. Putting on conferences and developing relationships all over the world is a natural fit for Gary.

These are the five major roles that are the serious commitments beyond volunteering and donations. Which one fits you?

Section Three

THE INSPIRATION OF SIGNIFICANCE

NINE

THE ELUSIVE NATURE OF SIGNIFICANCE

Meaning is not something you stumble across, like the answer to a riddle or the prize in a treasure hunt. Meaning is something you build into your life. You build it out of your own past, out of your affections and loyalties, out of the experience of humankind as it is passed on to you, out of your own talent and understanding, out of the things you believe in, out of the things and people you love, out of the values for which you are willing to sacrifice something. The ingredients are there. You are the only one who can put them together into that unique pattern that will be your life. Let it be a life that has dignity and meaning for you. If it does, then the particular balance of success or failure is of less account.
**Extracted from "The Road to Renewal,"
a speech given by John Gardner in April 1993**

Significance isn't about success or failure. It's about meaning. While success is most often externally defined—power, position, and property—meaning is entirely a matter of individual choice. It grows from within. What is meaningful to one has no value at all to another.

Meaning is what you build your life around. For example, making more money no longer means very much to me. Even though it was *central* to me in my First Half, it no longer strikes me as worth much except as a medium to pay for things that are more important to me now—like learning, like building relationships, like fulfilling the calling God has placed on my life. Why should I trade that which I have plenty of for that which I yet lack? That which I keep wishing I had more of?

You have expended a good deal of emotional and intellectual capital during the First Half of your professional life on a career that returned enough benefits to make the investment worthwhile. But during the past few years you have begun to question if you are really getting enough return on your investment. The money, status, and sense of contribution is no longer as strong as it was the day you drew your first paycheck. You sense that you were given your talents and abilities for something more, something beyond merely accumulating wealth. The "something beyond" is significance.

I cannot fully define significance for you except to say that in most cases it involves giving—giving away what is often most valuable to you. For most of us, that means a combination of money and time. When we invest these rich assets in others, we truly gain significance. We transcend the nettlesome and prosaic details of life as we settle into the lives we were meant to live.

Those of us who are fortunate enough to live in the developed world of the twenty-first century have a range of options unimagined to most of our predecessors and to almost all of the people still alive today. And for the most part, we take choice for granted. Like a fish swimming in water, we lose touch with the uniqueness of our environment. As Bill Moyers said in his 2000 commencement address at the University of Texas at Austin:

> If the earth's population shrunk to a village of
> precisely 100 people, with all the existing
> human ratios remaining the same, of the 100
> people, 57 would be Asians, 21 Europeans, 14
> would be from the Western Hemisphere (north
> and south) and 8 would be from Africa. Fifty-
> two would be female and 48 would be male.
> Seventy would have skin of color and 30 would
> be white. Seventy would not be Christian and
> 30 would. Eighty of the 100 would live in sub-
> standard housing. Seventy would be unable to
> read. Fifty would suffer from malnutrition.

The World Bank estimates that 46 percent of the
population of sub-Saharan Africa lived on less than $1 a
day in 1998, exactly what the percentage was in 1987.
These people have a very narrow range of options. They
don't have choices. We do. In fact, we are confronted with
the problem of *over*-choice. Hear this from the same John
Gardner speech quoted above:

> In the stable periods of history, meaning was
> supplied in the context of a coherent commu-
> nity and traditionally prescribed patterns of cul-
> ture. Today you can't count on any such
> heritage. You have to build meaning into your
> life, and you build it through your *commitments,*
> whether to your religion, to an ethical order as
> you conceive it, to your life's work, to loved
> ones, to your fellow humans. Young people run
> around searching for identity, but it isn't
> handed out free anymore—not in this transient,
> rootless, pluralistic society. Your identity is what
> you've committed yourself to.

In the Second Half, the second adulthood that the
affluence and longevity of our peculiar time and place has
granted us, we can choose to fashion a new identity of

significance based on a new set of commitments. But commit we must if we are not to squander this wonderful privilege and opportunity. Business as usual won't do. Neither will procrastination. This is the "later" we have been waiting for. It's either opportunity lost or opportunity gained. But either way, significance is a choice among options.

Sometimes, the only real reason people get stuck in Halftime is they have done everything but settle the question of significance. They want a change. Something new, perhaps more exciting. They have done all the exercises. Volunteered some time with various nonprofits. Consulted with friends and colleagues. Reengineered their lives so that they have the time and money to invest. Yet they have never fully *committed* to something of true significance.

The issue is really one of choice. Annie Dillard once wrote, "How we spend our days, of course, is how we spend our lives." You can choose to make Halftime a full-time hobby for the rest of your life. Or you can take the giant and sometimes scary leap of faith into the life you have always wanted. I don't think there's much doubt as to what you *want* to do. The real question is what *will* you do?

TEN

LEADING LEVEL 5 LIVES

You never conquer the mountain. You only conquer yourself.
Jim Whitaker, Everest climber

Significance is heroic, but not in the world's terms. It is only incidentally, if at all, about medals, honors, applause, rewards. In fact, these worldly symbols can be stumbling blocks, obstacles on the road to leading a meaningful life. These are things that can keep us stuck instead of moving us ahead. They can convince us that significance is like success—that personal significance is striving for a goal, some sort of summit that signifies final arrival and a release from responsibility. Yet the summit *always* leaves people feeling kind of empty.

When Lewis and Clark reached the Pacific Ocean after months of "undaunted courage" and hardship, they did get to celebrate for a moment ("Ocean in sight. Oh, what a joy!") but almost immediately there was winter and the long journey back to St. Louis. More Everest climbers die on the way down than up, summits are dangerous in more ways than one. It's not a good thing to be on the leeward side of your life. Merriweather Lewis never got over his grand achievement. He died a drunk and a suicide.

A life of significance is a long haul and it's a team sport. More like a relay race. Each of us plays only a small part acting as God's instruments in influencing the lives of others. It's been that way in my life.

My mother made sure I got to church. When I was a boy, a wise neighbor, Addison Sessions, taught Bible stories on late summer afternoons to a group of neighborhood kids growing up in Okmulgee, Oklahoma. Later as a young adult, Sug Bracken, who Billy Graham named as one of the two great women Bible teachers, carried me the next leg of my journey. Any number of people helped me in business. Peter Drucker has been the major figure in shaping the Second Half of my life. Alice Mae Harold, an ageless eighty-something African American woman is my prayer warrior. Each of these people has played a heroic role in my life—each in an utterly unique and pivotal way.

In many ways, the Second Half life that I envision is a lot like a series of stepping stones. Each of us becomes one rock that helps someone else get across the river. One of the ways Christianity differs from the world system (in theory if not always in practice) is that the world is pretty much a transactional quid pro quo way of going about life. I do one for you. You reciprocate by doing one for me. By contrast, the system Jesus taught is a circulatory system. The gift keeps on moving. You do something for me. I do something for the next person I find in need. As the apostle Paul once said to settle an argument:

> You are still worldly. For since there is jealousy and quarreling among you, are you not worldly? Are you not acting like mere men? For when one says, "I follow Paul," and another, "I follow Apollos," are you not mere men?
>
> What, after all, is Apollos? And what is Paul? Only servants, through whom you came to believe—as the Lord has assigned to each his

task. I planted the seed, Apollos watered it, but God made it grow. So neither he who plants nor he who waters is anything, but only God, who makes things grow.

1 Corinthians 3:3–7

No big deal. No credit. It's a different kind of heroism.

Yet even this has some parallels in the business world. Jim Collins, the brilliant researcher, who co-authored *Built to Last,* which some consider the best business book of the last decade, is finishing a new and fascinating project to determine what distinguishes companies that go from average to great. He has found that each of these great companies (there were only eleven "average to great" companies out of the 1,400 companies who have graced the *Fortune* 500 over the years) had a single dominant characteristic—they were led by what Collins calls a "Level 5 Executive." And in a speech to Leadership Network's "Exploring Off the Map" conference, he told us these exceptional people (he called them "the selfless executives") had two characteristics. First they were totally sold out to the work they were doing. Their ambitions *for the work* were unbounded. And second, Collins said each had the virtue of what he called "very deep personal humility." They were utterly comfortable with the idea that their successors would get the credit for the things they put in place. That sums up the Level 5 Executive.

In the Q&A following his lecture, I asked Collins how to apply this to having a great life. He responded with two questions worth thinking about:

- What is the difference between your real life purpose and what you're currently doing?
- What would it mean to be Level 5 in our lives?

Perhaps the best example of a Level 5 leader I have met was William E. Simon. I met him twice, once during the 1970s when he was U.S. Treasury Secretary and the speaker for a Dallas YPO event. He struck me then as a deeply principled, relentless workaholic, in many ways the quintessential on-task Wall Street hard driver. The second meeting was earlier this year. I had become friends with Bill Simon Jr., the forty-something son of this towering presence, very much his own person and, by my reckoning, a hero just like his dad. Linda and I shared a near perfect dinner with Bill and his sister, Mary Streep (yes, she is the sister-in-law of the actress) in one of those oh-so-splendid Manhattan restaurants. Afterwards, Bill invited Linda and me the next day to come by the New York offices of the John Olin Foundation to meet his father.

I found a man of the same relentless determination but in a frail physical package ravaged by the effect of a disease that proved to be terminal. You had a sense that he knew and that he was choosing very carefully how to allocate his remaining energy. Here's the way Bill Jr. described his father in a paper he later sent titled simply: "Dad—Eulogy Final Draft."

> Yes, Dad could be driven and demanding. But Dad also asked nothing of others that he wasn't already demanding of himself.
>
> It's been said that we make a living by what we get but we make a life by what we give. And what a life he made, because there were no limits to what he would give for the four great pillars in his life: Family...Friends...Freedom... and Faith.

Bill went on to describe the first three themes. When he came to the last, here's what he said:

Dad was a warrior. To my knowledge he never shied from a discussion, debate, or even an argument in his entire life. He defined his life by the convictions he held and the battles he fought.

But in his later years he enlisted his legendary energies in a new, some would say, uncharacteristic, way.

Dad signed on as a foot soldier for Jesus Christ...he fought in the war where victory is actually won by surrendering...to God...and where the weapons of faith are deployed in heart-to-heart combat to save the sick, the poor, and the forgotten.

How proud we were to see our dad become a Eucharistic minister. At Cardinal Cooke, at Morristown Memorial, at Sloane Kettering, at Cottage Hospital. Wherever his travels would take him.

Dad was an inspiring example. As he padded down those halls day after day, ministering and praying with men, women, and children whose eyes beseeched him for company and comfort.

He flew down to Texas with Chuck Colson to help bring God to prisoners on death row where they prayed with grown men just before they walked that last mile.

So, this is how he wrote his last glorious chapter:

A man who loved his family more than words could ever say ...

A man loyal to a fault to every one of his friends ...

A man who fought for freedom every day of his life ...

And a man who introduced God to those who needed him most.

My father lived a wonderful life. One lived in deeds, not years. Where what he did, not only touched but quite often transformed the lives of so many people all across the world.

With his restless intellectual curiosity, he never once stopped trying to learn or stopped caring about those four pillars in his life; family, faith, friends and freedom and his legacy will be a beacon for generations to come.

And now, Dad has reached the dawn of a new life. If we could ask him how he was doing–no doubt he would say two words, "Terrific pal!"

Now that's my vision of a Level 5 life: totally sold out to his deepest values, balanced with a spirit of deep humility. It is what I see being approached by those who have successfully entered the Second Half, and it is what I am just now beginning to experience myself. It is not dependent upon money or stature or title, but instead is the product of aligning our lives and talents with the God who gave us both.

ELEVEN

THE NEED FOR A HEROIC SECOND HALF

[Man] has to feel and believe that what he is doing is truly heroic, timeless, and supremely meaningful.

Ernest Becker

If the First Half of your career is about conquest, the Second Half is about heroism (or despair for the lack of it). In the First Half you were driven by the need to provide, to achieve. You had a family to provide for, a career to establish, a mountain to climb. Now that you've gotten to the top—or as close to it as you ever will—the conquest isn't as important as it once was. Your motives have changed, along with life's circumstances. As your children mature and approach adulthood themselves, you begin to wonder: What will my legacy be to them? How will I be remembered? You are more interested in impact than assets.

Much of life is the quest for the heroic. From the time we first begin playing in the backyard to the present, one of the inner drives that motivates our behavior is the need to stand above the crowd. At the midpoint in our lives, however, its attraction is the strongest.

I believe this quest for the heroic is behind much of what *Time* magazine (July 24, 2000) calls "The New Philanthropy." It is what drove Bill Gates to give away $22 billion and Ted Turner more than a billion. For the mega-wealthy, it is a way of leaving a legacy—a permanent handprint on the planet. For those who are not in that class of billionaires, we look for other ways to leave a mark on the world.

It is a good thing, this desire to be a hero. It is, in my opinion, a God-inspired calling to a higher plane of living.

In my generation, especially growing up in Texas, young boys looked up to heroic figures like Gary Cooper and James Stewart, graduating later to Douglas MacArthur and Winston Churchill. We had sports heroes like Mickey Mantle and Roger Staubach and Bob Cousy, and we looked to great presidents like Eisenhower and Kennedy as heroic models.

Heroes beget heroes. We look to the heroic figure for qualities that we want to emulate. It is the hero who teaches us about courage and bravery and wisdom and compassion. Some of my early heroes were from the Bible. In grade school my mother and father had moved from East Texas to Okmulgee, Oklahoma, to own and operate a small radio station (everything was small in Okmulgee, but it looked "big" to me at the time). Our next-door neighbor was a larger-than-life raconteur named Addison Sessions who would gather the neighborhood kids late in the afternoon to tell us Bible stories—mostly Old Testament. Those characters formed me and they still live in my mind. Joseph leading the kingdom of Egypt. David slaying Goliath. Abraham leading his journey of faith to the Promised Land. Moses and the Exodus. They followed God on great adventures, and they touched my boyish heart as examples of men taking action based on their faith—I wanted to be like them someday.

It is in the Second Half of life that we have the greatest opportunity to be truly heroic. Not just play like motion picture heroes but the real thing. The yearning for significance is really the desire to be remembered for something that counts. It is what you are feeling when the promotion and raise just don't turn your crank like they used to. And in God's perfect sense of timing, he has released us through affluence and longevity from the necessity of spending our every waking moment either earning the symbols of success or diverting ourselves from the cares and concerns of the world and the deceitfulness of riches: the two primary preoccupations of the First Half of life. The Second Half is where we can be self-consciously heroic by "giving up our life for our friends." The Bible demands this and says life is meaningless—a clanging symbol—without it. And perhaps most important from a practical sense, the teaching and life of Christ gives us legitimacy in this quest for the heroic. In the Second Half of life we begin to understand that being a hero is more about who we are than what we do.

In his Pulitzer prize-winning book, *The Denial of Death,* Ernest Becker states that "we like to be reminded that our central calling, our main task on this planet, is the heroic." He equates the call to be heroic with the quest for significance, or what he calls "a feeling of primary value, of cosmic specialness, of ultimate usefulness to creation, of lasting worth and meaning."

When you were fresh out of college, you wanted to be a hero to your parents, perhaps to a girlfriend or spouse, to anyone with whom you had a personal relationship. You wanted to stand out, to be noticed, and the primary way to do that when you are young is to get a decent job and begin keeping score in tangible ways you could point to: a large salary, a prominent position with the right firm, promotions, and possessions. Becker calls these "structures of statuses and roles, customs, and rules of behavior."

In many ways I believe we have mislabeled those who display their success as materialistic. In effect, they are just trying to be heroes, a desire that Becker says is as natural as it is good. Try to recall the first time you came home from work with news that you had received a raise. Naturally, you wanted to tell your spouse as soon as possible, to celebrate this achievement. Were you succumbing to materialism and greed? I don't think so at all. At that moment, you were a hero to your spouse. She looked at you admiringly because she too understood the "structures of statuses and roles, customs, and rules for behavior."

But ultimately, you began to understand the shallowness of these heroic symbols. If you were raised in the Christian tradition, you had collected a lifetime of warnings about the inability of these symbols to provide happiness and fulfillment, so it made sense when those feelings of restlessness started to settle in. Each promotion and raise tantalized you with a temporary feeling of the heroic—by now you had a family to pat you on the back and celebrate with you—and a bigger house or more prestigious car elicited a certain awe that felt like hero worship. But it passed so quickly into a form of servitude: Instead of making you a hero, your success was turning you into a slave.

I think we have been too hard on our culture and ourselves. Clearly we have all accumulated too much stuff, but I do not really believe our instincts were morally corrupt, as some would have us believe. Everyone wants to be a hero. And once we recognize this, it will help us progress on our journey into the Second Half. For if we are willing to admit that what we really want is to be a hero, the Second Half becomes even more appealing. It is the one place where true heroism thrives.

What is it about our Bible stories that are so appealing? These are stories of men and women doing extraordinary things by conquering the fears, the needs for comfort and security that seem to hold the rest of us back from doing the work God prompts us to do. Nehemiah rebuilding the walls of Jerusalem, Noah building the ark, Moses leading the Exodus, Gideon routing the enemy, Esther saving her people.

Joseph Campbell defines a hero as one who is given over to a cause that is larger than himself. Heroism is about the ability some men and women have to transcend themselves, to put themselves at risk in response to a sense of calling. It's what Jesus meant when he spoke of losing your life in order to gain your life. In that sense, Jesus was the ultimate hero...the one who was always obedient to his Father's mission.

We try in the First Half and generally fail to achieve true heroism. Previous generations could not very easily expect a second chance to be a hero. But in God's great providence he has placed us in a time where we really *can* choose a different path for the Second Half. He has given us an economy of health and money that allows us this freedom to be a hero for his sake.

You cannot be a hero by continuing to play by the self-interested rules of the First Half. You need to follow the universal example of all our heroes: They took a chance, defied the odds, went up against conventional wisdom, and forged ahead despite the warnings. It is both frightening and energizing, but it is what leads to significance.

TWELVE
WHAT DO YOU WANT TO BE REMEMBERED FOR?

Peter Drucker relates this story in his book *Managing the Non-Profit Organization:*

> When I was thirteen, I had an inspiring teacher of religion, who one day went right through the class of boys asking each one, "What do you want to be remembered for?" None of us, of course, could give an answer. So, he chuckled and said, "I didn't expect you to be able to answer it. But if you can't answer it by the time you're fifty, you will have wasted your life." We eventually had a sixtieth reunion of that high school class. Most of us were still alive, but we hadn't seen each other since we graduated, and so the talk at first was a little stilted. Then one of the fellows asked, "Do you remember Father Pfliegler and that question?" We all remembered it. And each one said it had made all the difference to him, although they didn't really understand that until they were in their forties.
>
> At twenty-five, some of us began trying to answer it and, by and large, answered it foolishly. Joseph Schumpeter, one of the greatest

economists of this century, claimed at twenty-five that he wanted to be remembered as the best horseman in Europe, the greatest lover in Europe, and as a great economist. By age sixty, just before he died, he was asked the question again. He no longer talked of horsemanship and he no longer talked of women. He said he wanted to be remembered as the man who had given an early warning of the dangers of inflation. That is what he is remembered for—and it's worthwhile being remembered for. Asking that question changed him, even though the answer he gave at twenty-five was singularly stupid, even for a man of twenty-five.

I'm always asking that question: What do you want to be remembered for? It is a question that induces you to renew yourself, because it pushes you to see yourself as a different person—the person you can *become*. If you are fortunate, someone with the moral authority of a Father Pfliegler will ask you that question early enough in your life so that you will continue to ask it as you go through life.

Halftime is the time when we need to be asking ourselves that question in the most earnest and serious manner possible. For people who are followers of Christ, conversion is of ultimate importance and would probably qualify as an appropriate generic answer. But be more specific. What do *you* want to be remembered for?

Eighty-five percent of Americans consider themselves to be Christian. Over 30 percent define themselves as "born again."

Hopefully, this question of belief is a First Half question, that is, one that you have settled early in life whether Christian or some other way. It represents the first passage of faith: from unbelief to belief. If this first passage is based, as I believe it is, on truth and not just hopeful fantasy, then it is the most important step for anyone to take.

My own first passage came when I was quite young. The idea that there was a God who created the world and a Christ who was sent to compensate for the obvious behavioral shortfall of us human beings made sense to me almost from the beginning. It wasn't a dramatic event. For me, faith came as a gift from God. My decision was whether to receive the gift or not. Belief, for me anyway, is as natural a part of life as breathing.

But there is what I call "the second passage" that receives far less attention from religious bodies, the passage from faith to works; from belief to commitment; from latent energy (the innate capacity to do good) to active energy; from seed to fruit. This second passage has been the concern of my midlife journey from success to significance.

In business we are used to being asked, "What's the end game?" "What's the bottom line?" "What am I being held accountable for?" Most of us think we know what that means in our job, but we're unaccustomed to answering that question in our personal lives. When we ask in a Halftime seminar (see *www.Halftime.org*) whether people have a mission statement for their business, most of the hands go up. When we ask whether people have a *personal* mission statement written down, very few raise their hands.

I read the book of Ecclesiastes at least once a year. It is the classic text of existential philosophy by a man who experienced life fully. Solomon, the wisest figure in the Old Testament opens this wisdom book with this question, "What advantage does man have in all his work which he does under the sun?" In other words: What's the profit? What's left over at the end of the game?

Life on this earth will end, and when it does I visualize what I call "The Final Exam." It is where the sheep will be separated from the goats. The way I see it, there will be two questions: (1) What did you do about Jesus—did you accept Jesus in terms of his own profession about himself or did you turn your back and walk away? (2) What did you do with what I gave you to work with? Not Billy Graham, not Pope John Paul II or your priest or Mother Teresa, but *you?* The answer can't be delegated by writing a check once a year to "organized religion." It's personal.

The Bible teaches that each of us has been equipped with special gifts that are as unique as our fingerprints. I call it our Spiritual DNA and the New Testament tells us that it is as well-defined as the physical DNA that determines whether we are male or female. Each of us is called by God to use this gift to serve others. This is what we all will be held accountable for on the final exam—the highest accountability for our lives here on earth. Even higher and more enduring than the answer to Peter Drucker's question, "What do I want to be remembered for?" After all, memory fades, eternity lasts.

At best, I expect to be remembered for a few years from the time that I die. I remember asking Curtis Meadows, who for fifteen years ran the $800 million Meadows Foundation, the largest private foundation in Dallas and the one everybody else looks to for leadership, how long it takes for heirs to begin making their own plans. I asked naively, "Is it a couple of years, maybe five?" He said, "The next morning!"—three words that have remained imprinted in my memory ever since.

Given that reality, I have plans to invest most of what I own in high-yield kingdom enterprises in the next fifteen years while I still have the interest and energy to be personally involved. I call it "high-yield/right-now philanthropy" to distinguish it from the government-mandated 5 percent a year variety that characterizes most foundations. At age seventy-five I will take another look and hope I have the energy and passion to do more.

Meanwhile, I want to find the 100X multiplier entrepreneurs who are doing God's work *right now* and get my capital and knowledge compounding for good. Discounted cash flow works both ways. Not only is a dollar received fifteen years from now worth a lot less than today, but a dollar invested in God's work today will compound over a period of years in the hands of one of the kingdom entrepreneurs I have come to know through Leadership Network. Multiply it out. One dollar invested today grows to $100 if compounded at 15 percent per year over a thirty-five-year career of a 100X kingdom entrepreneur. I have done 100X in business and certainly hope I can do it in God's work as well. I am certain it can be done, but I have concluded that I pretty much have to do it myself—at least in the sense of being as active personally in picking where to place my shots and working these kingdom investments for 100X yield. I want my equivalent of the five loaves and two fishes to feed thousands. There's little question that I'm more ambitious in my Second Half than I was in my First Half. The stakes are larger.

I am more interested in yield management—increasing the yield on my life for God's kingdom than I am in "sin management." I hope the quest for yield will "crowd out" my natural instinct for sin. (I bought a black T-shirt at the Museum of Modern Art in New York that has red letters on the front, "I too have sinned," to remind me of my capacities in that category of life.)

So I have a problem, what my business friends call a "high-class problem." I want a lot of yield for these dollars and for the time I will invest. I want to be remembered as a high-yield/right-now philanthropist and kingdom entrepreneur.

I could certainly get rid of the money quickly at most any big university, but that is not the route I feel called to take. What I call high-yield/right-now philanthropy implies a proactive approach to investing my Second Half capital just as high-yield investing did in my First Half business career. I treat it as a calling and consider the enduring legacy of my life only that which is poured into the lives of others. That's where the multiplication is and the opportunity is *now*.

Andrew Carnegie, the steel magnate, who, with Rockefeller, practically invented American philanthropy, reasoned there were only three places his excess capital could go. He could overendow his children and, in the process, remove their incentives to achieve. He could pass the money on to his lawyer or other paid executor of his estate to invest in good works as *they* saw fit. Or he could invest the money in good causes in his lifetime, guiding his legacy to others with the entrepreneurial skills learned in his First Half.

He chose to do the latter and he touched millions of lives. That's the path I intend to take.

I want to compound the gifts of intellectual, relational, and financial capital God has given me to work with, and I want to do it in my lifetime. It's *my* responsibility. It's what I will be held accountable for when I face *my* final exam.

You have different gifts and a different responsibility. Perhaps you are a teacher or a caregiver. Maybe you have the gift of prayer or the gift of hospitality. This matter of calling is highly individual. Of this I am certain, God will only hold each of us accountable for the gifts he has given us individually to work with. But he *will* hold each of us accountable—one at a time.

What did you do about Jesus? Did you accept him or did you turn away from him?

What will you do with what God has given you to work with? With *your* knowledge? With *your* relational network? With *your* financial resources? With the passions of *your* heart?

The consequences of your answers stretch across eternity. This life is just a test for the better one to come. Eternity *is* longer than time. Much longer.

> One goes through it all to arrive at faith, the faith that one's very creatureliness has some meaning to a Creator; that despite one's true insignificance, weakness, death, one's existence has meaning in some ultimate sense because it exists within an eternal and infinite scheme of things brought about and maintained to some kind of design by some creative force.
>
> **Ernest Becker**

THIRTEEN

THE END OF THE BEGINNING

*What we call the beginning is often the end and to
make an end is to make a beginning. The end is
where we start from ...*
  But to what purpose ...
Let me disclose the gift reserved for age
  To set a crown on your lifetime's effort ...
*What you thought you came for is only a shell, a husk
of meaning from which the purpose breaks only when
it is fulfilled ...*
  *For us, there is only the trying. The rest is not
  our business.*
T. S. Eliot, "Four Quartets"

As I have attempted to say in the introduction and
throughout this book—something new is happening. It is
so new that people don't know quite how to respond to it
yet. So a lot of people are "stuck" in the face of this new
opportunity.

What used to be the end of adult life followed by a
short period that was essentially waiting to die has now
been replaced by what I call the Second Half. This second
adulthood of twenty or thirty years for most of us is best
characterized by three words (you can remember them
as AOL):

A...Affluence

O...Options

L...Longevity

This is personal opportunity, a civic opportunity, and a kingdom opportunity. The opportunity can either be squandered in idleness or it can be the capstone of a life well lived. For me the Second Half has become a new beginning—a chance to multiply the knowledge, the relational network, and the financial resources that my First Half has generated into a life of contribution and not merely a life of accumulation. Perhaps in some strange way my not having the only son Linda and I lost at age twenty-four saves me from the temptation to dump the money and the responsibility in Ross's lap, diverting him from whatever course he might have chosen for himself. I don't know. These things are for me to discover in heaven, not now.

This I *do* know—for me Halftime has been the end of the beginning of my Second Half. And the Second Half seems from this vantage point to be what my life has been all about. People talk of "legacy." That could well be an outcome of what I am doing now, but I don't think of it in that way. Calling. Destiny. Responsibility. These are the words that have a truer ring to me.

And I believe those are words that will increasingly pull at the hearts of those of us blessed to have lived during these decades of prosperity and opportunity. We have been given more than any generation in history: more wealth, more possessions, more freedom, more time. By themselves, though, these unprecedented benefits do not fully satisfy that deep longing that God has placed within each of us to count. To matter. To be needed. To be remembered.

Many religious leaders have quoted the words of Jesus, "To whom much is given, much is also required," and always the impression is given that this is almost a punishment for being richly blessed. I don't think that was our Lord's intent at all. Rather, he knew that the greatest of all virtues is charity: giving something away to receive even more. More that cannot be measured with ledger sheets but with lives who are changed by our actions.

I am convinced that once you clearly see your calling, the details will fall in place because you will be so energized by what the future holds for you. You will have seen a glimpse of how the qualities that make you unique match the needs that are waiting specifically for you, and it will be enough to get you out of the rut.

If Peter Drucker has taught me anything, it is that no one can predict the future, much less control it. The future—at least the future that remains after I have gone on to the final, eternal, and *best* season of my life (heaven)—is in the hands of God and those who will inhabit this planet in my absence—my concerns are all with what I can do *right now*—I can have some control or at least influence on what Peter calls "the futurity of present events." I can use the gifts God has given me to work with *now*. Now, not years from now.

And that is my parting challenge to you. It is time. Right now! Today! You cannot afford to wait another day to obey that still, small voice inside that is calling you to get on with it—this new beginning that is the doorway to the best years of your life. No amount of golf or travel or endless dinners in exotic locations will ever match the excitement of significance. I have been doing this for over fifteen years now, and I can say with absolute certainty:

The best is yet to be if you are willing to break away from the pack.

So do it now! Don't wait until you have everything worked out in a perfect plan, because that plan may never materialize. Don't hold back because you don't have enough money or you are afraid your phone will never ring if your current title is dropped from your name. You will, and it will.

Don't wait until the end of the fiscal year or until your employer can find your replacement or until you've had a chance to travel a little. Those are distractions that can keep your Second Half life on hold permanently.

The still, small voice you are hearing is the same voice that spoke to a young boy named Samuel. At first, he thought it was the voice of a man under whom he was serving. But it was the voice of God. And the voice said to Samuel, "I am about to do something that will make the ears of everyone who hears of it tingle."

That is what you are hearing as you approach the Second Half of your life. If you obey, you will "make the ears of everyone who hears of it tingle."

It is just that exciting!

ABOUT DISCOURAGEMENT

One of the great living saints I have had the inexpressible pleasure of knowing personally was Henri Nouwen, the late Catholic writer and priest who many think inherited the mantle of Thomas Merton. Henri was gracious enough to endorse my first book, *Halftime.*

One evening at dinner with my wife, Linda, and me in Ft. Worth, Henri told us that he thought there was a stage *after* significance. Henri called this final stage, "surrender." He meant giving your life over to God.

He said he had thought a lot about it since reading *Halftime* and that he had concluded that one couldn't really go from success to surrender without passing through significance; that there would be too much anger, a natural inner response to giving up success as life's organizing principle.

Since then I have read a good deal more of Henri's work. He describes himself as a "wounded healer." He frequently found himself plagued by days of depression. In the language of this book, he was sometimes "stuck." Yet *he always pressed on.* His life, especially in his latter years when I knew him, personified surrender.

I too have days of discouragement. Disappointments in people—in myself! Plans that do not work out.

Significance → Surrender (final stage)

The antidote—the only antidote—which keeps these gray times from piling up into despair for me is to look upward and to look outward—to build on the islands of health and strength ignoring the sea of ineptitude that characterizes so much well-intended human endeavor.

"Trust in the Lord with all your heart and lean not on your own understanding." This verse from Proverbs meant so much to me standing on a bluff over the Rio Grande River as the fact sunk into me that I would never see my twenty-four-year-old son again until we meet in heaven. It is still a central reality for me. There is so much I cannot understand with the limited capacities of my rational mind.

The other antidote to pain that I learned during the time I was grieving so intensely over the loss of my son was that it *always* provided temporary symptomatic relief for me to focus on the problems of someone else, to take the center of attention away from myself, to listen to another and attempt to find some way to serve. And in this I am encouraged to find that the great saints, the classical spiritual writers were similarly strengthened. Here's the voice of Saint Teresa of Avilà, the sixteenth-century Spanish writer of *The Interior Castle:*

> If we go astray at the beginning and want the Lord to do our will and lead us as *our* desires dictate, how can we build on a firm foundation? I must remind you that it is the Lord's will that we should be tested....
>
> If, then, you sometimes fall, do not lose heart. Even more, do not cease striving to make progress from it, for even out of your fall God will bring some good....The only way to lose is to turn back.

"Stuck" is not a one-time event that you can "fix," then, having surmounted it, press forward without further difficulty. Stuck happens over and over again.

So as I find myself discouraged and stuck once more, I think of Henri, I think of Saint Teresa. I think of the apostle Paul on his difficult journey. I think of Jesus. And I press on whether I feel like it or not. I trust in the Lord. I attempt once more to pour myself into someone else's life. I lose my life of discouragement and gain my life once again.

It is a miracle. Here comes another day!

ACKNOWLEDGEMENTS

Thinking that we can do things on our own is an egocentric myth, a conceit that keeps us from acknowledging and celebrating how utterly we are a part of one another's lives. As I reflect on it, my debts to others are numberless and in a constant state of varying intensity depending on what's going on in my life and work.

My deepest debts are to my wife, Linda, for the love and affection we have shared for thirty-nine years of marriage, and to Peter Drucker for the inspiration and encouragement he has given me to live for significance in the Second Half of my life, as well as his unfailing ability to "see" the landscape of our world so clearly. Peter has been my guide, as Virgil was for Dante.

For my three books, my deepest debt is to Lyn Cryderman, who has colabored with me over every word. The thoughts are mine, but Lyn so often found the better way to express the ideas I am trying to get across and to sequence them properly. The word "conspire," whose root words mean to "breathe together," describes our relationship in this work.

My thanks go to those I work with in Leadership Network, Leadership Training Network, Halftime, VentureWorks, and the Peter F. Drucker Foundation for Nonprofit Management, the organizational vehicles through which I now work. Thanks especially to Beryl Berry, Gayle Carpenter, B J Engle, Carol Childress, Lisa Cummins, Colleen Hager, Mike McMahon, Jason Mitchell, Warren Schuh, Brad Smith, Dave Travis, Greg Ligon, Greg Murtha, Heather Hyde, Ken Jennings, Rob Johnston, and the indefatigable Frances Hesselbein.

These organizations have been strengthened immeasurably by dedicated and wise board members: John Findley, Merle Smith, Jack Willome, and Walt Wilson for Leadership Network; John DiIulio, Wally Hawley, Christine Letts, Lloyd Reeb, and Bob Shank for Halftime; and to the Board of Governers of The Drucker Foundation, especially David Beatty, Richard Cavanagh, Doris Drucker, Marshall Goldsmith, Geneva Johnson, John McNeice Jr., Thomas Moran, Bill Pollard, Richard Schubert, and Iain Somerville. An award of exceptional merit goes to Doris Drucker whose stated mission is "the preservation of Peter Drucker." *Forbes* magazine declared on its cover that Peter Drucker, at age ninety, was "still the youngest mind." Nice work, Doris!

The Buford Foundation would be entrusted to its board: Linda Buford, John Castle, Tom Luce, and Don Williams. I can't imagine better friends and wiser advisors. I have vowed to spend the rest of my life with smart virtuous people who are doing things that make a difference. These four people personify that wish.

And first and last, there is God. I can only hope that this has been God's work. I resonate with the words of David in Psalm 139 when he says:

> O Lord, you have searched me
> And you know me.
> You know when I sit and when I rise;
> You perceive my thought from afar.
> You discern my going out and my lying down;
> You are familiar with all my ways.
> Before a word is on my tongue

You know it completely, O Lord.
You hem me in—behind and before;
You have laid your hand upon me.
Such knowledge is too wonderful for me,
Too lofty for me to attain.

Good job, God! I'm happy to have been along for the ride. What's next?

APPENDIX

**A "Toolkit of Resources" for those who
want to drill deeper
(also available at www.Halftime.org)**
Recommended by Bob Buford

PROGRAMS

The Master's Program—A three-year life coaching program

"A dream without a plan is a fantasy," according to Bob Shank, originator and developer of the Master's Program. In a three-year life coaching program, participants team with each other and a facilitator/coach to identify their unique abilities and God's design for their life. Using a variety of tools and teaching materials, the participant learns how to get control of his or her life and time and realize life mastery in all realms of life: personal, family, professional, and kingdom. Delivered through twelve full-day sessions over the course of three years, TMP has brought clarity and significant life-change to those who have already completed the course. For more information and locations, please contact by phone at 949–646–5874 or by e-mail at mastersprogram@aol.com.

Halftime Zondervan *Groupware*™—Video with participant's guide

This five-part video series with participant's discussion guide explores the questions, decisions, and feelings associated with the Halftime experience. Featuring men and women from all walks of life, it is an excellent resource for use in a church, office, or neighborhood small group or retreat. It converts the book, *Halftime,* into a conversation with friends and peers. (*www.Haltime.org*)

The Strategic Coach

This is a powerful process that enables experienced, successful entrepreneurs to
1) dramatically increase free time
2) increase focus on their most important results-producing relationships and centers of influence
3) delegate "stuff" and clean up "messes" in their lives that interfere with productivity
4) build a team that frees them up to develop their unique talents and abilities. (*info@strategiccoach.com*)

Wise Counsel

This is a practical, "how to, nuts and bolts" process of twelve local Christian Entrepreneurs/Executives who meet monthly and learn through noted experts and fellow leaders. They share wisdom and advise on business and ministry decisions, as an outside board. This growing national network is led locally by a professional who meets regularly with each participant. Members encourage, support, and challenge one another in their bond to pursue their highest calling in the Second Half of life. For more information, please contact by phone at 904–268–0976 or by fax at 904–268–5223. (*www.wisecounselonline.com*)

BOOKS

Halftime, by Bob Buford

Halftime focuses on the important time of transition—the time when, as Buford says, a person moves beyond the First Half of the game of life. Midlife. Halftime. Buford provides the encouragement and insight to propel your life on a new course away from mere success to true significance—and the best years of your life. There's a new hard cover printing now available. (*www.amazon.com*)

Game Plan, by Bob Buford

This book answers the question "How do I move from success to significance in the Second Half of my life?" It highlights the need for a game plan, and provides a rough map to help you navigate your journey. (*www.amazon.com*)

Balancing Life's Demands, by J. Grant Howard

This book challenges the traditional, sequential approach to priorities (i.e., God is first in my life, someone else is second, etc.), offering a drastically different, thoroughly biblical and intensely practical solution. Includes personal illustrations, charts, and diagrams. (*www.amazon.com*)

Believers in Business, by Laura L. Nash

An amazing compilation of stories Dr. Nash learned by interviewing Christian CEOs. A top-flight resource for discussion and study groups as well as introspection. Now at Harvard Divinity School, Dr. Nash previously taught ethics at Harvard Business School. (*www.amazon.com*)

Business as a Calling: Work and the Examined Life, by Michael Novak

Why do we work so hard at our jobs, day after day? Why is a job well done important to us? We know there is more to a career than money and prestige, but what exactly do we mean by "fulfillment"? These are old but important questions. They belong with some newly discovered ones: Why are people in business more religious than the population as a whole? What do people of business know, and what do they do, that anchors their faith? In this groundbreaking and inspiring book, Michael Novak ties together these crucial questions by explaining the meaning of work as a vocation. Work should be more than just a job—it should be a calling. (*www.amazon.com*)

Celebration of Discipline, by Richard J. Foster

When Richard Foster began writing *Celebration of Discipline* more than twenty years ago, an older writer gave him a bit of advice: "Be sure that every chapter forces the reader into the next chapter." Foster took the advice to heart; as a result, his book presents one of the most compelling and readable visions of Christian spirituality published in the past few decades. (*www.amazon.com*)

Connecting, by Larry Crabb

Expands on his lifelong work in the field of psychotherapy to adopt a groundbreaking, but biblical, approach to healing the deep wounds of the soul–an approach that centers around building intimate, healing mini communities in our lives and churches. What we need is connection! What we need is a healing community! *Inside Out* by the same author is also excellent. (*www.amazon.com*)

Discontinuity and Hope: Radical Change and the Path to the Future, **by Lyle E. Schaller**

Change: Is that a good thing or a bad thing? That depends, says Lyle Schaller, on your viewpoint and values. Any given change can be threatening if all your values are wedded to the way things are now, if you can only view the future through the lens of the past. Or it can be exciting if your viewpoint is geared toward the new possibilities that will arise from this change. By looking at several examples of large-scale, discontinuous changes that have occurred over the last ten to thirty years, Schaller prepares church leaders to orient themselves to the new challenges and opportunities for ministry that will result from the accelerated transition going on around us. (*www.amazon.com*)

Experiencing God, **by Henry Blackaby**

This book shows you how to deepen your own personal relationship with God and discover your special place in his kingdom. Believers will renew and revitalize their love for the Lord by seeing his love for them in its full dimension. Available as a book, a devotional journal, or a workbook for personal or group studies. (*www.amazon.com*)

Finding a Job You Can Love, **by Ralph Mattson and Arthur Miller**

This book will help you identify those inherent gifts (talents) you possess and will give you specific insights into how best to apply them. Not only helpful on a personal level, but as a business tool since many organizations do not reach full potential because they lack the ability to tap into and utilize the unique talents of the people serving in the organization. This book provides a proven, effective means of doing that. (*www.amazon.com*)

High Performance Nonprofit Organizations, by Christine W. Letts, Allen Grossman, and William P. Ryan

Nonprofit organizations are now being forced to manage their activities in a more professional and corporate fashion, yet sometimes lack the solid guidance to make smooth transitions into these new management techniques. This unique book clearly and concisely shows nonprofits how to make general business management guidance relevant and effective by providing a framework for analyzing management and by translating business lingo into an accessible vocabulary for nonprofit managers. Christine W. Letts (Cambridge, MA) is a professor at the Kennedy School of Government at Harvard University. Allen Grossman (Garrison, NY) works with Outward Bound USA. William P. Ryan (Cambridge, MA) is a management consultant. (*www.amazon.com*)

Leader to Leader, by Frances Hesselbein and Paul M. Cohen

An inspiring examination of mission, leadership, values, innovation, building collaborations, shaping effective institutions, and creating community. Management pioneer Peter F. Drucker, Southwest Airlines CEO Herb Kelleher, best-selling authors Warren Bennis, Stephen Covey, and Charles Handy, Pulitzer prize winner Doris Kearns Goodwin, Harvard professors Rosabeth Moss Kanter and Regina Herslinger, and learning organization expert Peter Senge are among those who share their knowledge and experience in this essential resource. Their essays will spark ideas, open doors, and inspire all those who face the challenge of leading in an ever-changing environment. (*www.josseybass.com*)

Leadership by the Book, by Ken Blanchard, Bill Hybels, and Phil Hodges

Told in the parable format of *The One Minute Manager(s)* and *Raving Fans, Leadership by the Book* draws on the model and messages of Jesus as the source of practical lessons in effective leadership. Recounting the story of a teacher, a minister, and a marketplace leader who support one another in their leadership challenges, this extraordinary book offers unexpected and exceptional answers to tough leadership issues. (*www.amazon.com*)

Leadership Is an Art, by Max DePree

In what has become a bible for the business world, the successful CEO of Herman Miller, Inc. explores how executives and managers can learn the leadership skills that build a better, more profitable organization. This revolutionary and thoughtful book offers an innovative style of business leadership—a humanistic approach that is responsible for the remarkable success of some of America's most admired and best-managed companies. A book of ideas more than practices liberating people to do what is required of them in the most effective and humane way possible. (*www.amazon.com*)

The Life@Work Journal

Periodicals published bi-monthly by The Life@ Work Company, this excellent magazine serves as a resource for facilitating the integration of spiritual life and work. To order subscriptions, call toll free 877–543–9675, or email subscriptions@lifeatwork.com.

Living the Life You Were Meant to Live, by Tom Paterson

The principles taken from the LifePlanning™ Process, which has impacted America's top executives and ministry leaders for more than twenty years, will help you direct your efforts toward greater purpose and fulfillment; discover your foremost traits and talents; and balance the five domains of life: Personal, Family, Faith, Vocation, and Community. (*www.amazon.com*)

Managing the Non-Profit Organization, by Peter F. Drucker

The service, or non-profit, sector of our society is growing rapidly (with more than eight million employees and more than eighty million volunteers), creating a major need for guidelines and expert advice on how to manage these organizations effectively. Drucker gives examples and explanations of mission, leadership, resources, marketing, goals, people development, decision making, and much more. Included are interviews with nine experts that address key issues in the non-profit sector. (*www.pfdf.org; www.amazon.com*)

Management Challenges for the 21ˢᵗ Century, by Peter F. Drucker

In his first major new book since *Post-Capitalist Society,* Peter discusses the new paradigms of management, how they have changed and will continue to change our basic assumptions about the practices and principles of management. Peter shows how to be a leader in a period of change and explains the "new information revolution." He addresses the ultimate challenge of managing yourself while still meeting the demands on the individual during a longer working life and in an everchanging workplace. (*www.pfdf.org*)

Margin, by Richard A. Swenson

Overload is not having time to finish the book you're reading on stress. Margin is having time to read it twice. Overload is fatigue. Margin is energy. Overload is red ink. Margin is black ink. Overload is hurry. Margin is calm. Overload is anxiety. Margin is security. Overload is the disease of the 90s. Margin is the cure. (*www.amazon.com*)

The Millionaire Next Door, by Thomas J. Stanley and William D. Danko

You will learn seven common denominators that show up again and again among those who have accumulated wealth. Using two decades' worth of surveys, interviews, and data available nowhere else, this book gives you a detailed picture of who the rich are and how they live that will change forever your perception of what being wealthy really means. (*www.amazon.com*)

Mornings with Henri J. M. Nouwen

Readings and reflections. Henri Nouwen was one of the most popular, yet profound spiritual writers of our time. A priest, psychologist, and famed professor, Nouwen struggled to reconcile the paradoxes inherent in life and the Christian faith. This book touches upon the themes that defined his life: prayer, solitude, community, and the unlimited love of God. (*www.amazon.com*)

The Paradox of Success: When Winning at Work Means Losing at Life, by John R. O'Neil and Jeremy Tarcher

For leaders who are dissatisfied with what success has brought them and seek deep learning and renewal. In a lively and inviting style, a well-known consultant to troubled business executives draws upon fascinating psychological and business strategies to show the way out of this dilemma. (*www.amazon.com*)

The Path, by Laurie Beth Jones

Laurie Beth Jones tackles one of today's hottest topics–mission statements. Applicable to both personal and professional life, she teaches readers how to formulate a succinct, focused plan of action as a path to follow through life and in work. (*www.amazon.com*)

The Spirit of the Disciplines: Understanding How God Changes Lives, by Dallas Willard

This wise and compelling meditation invites us to a new understanding that sees salvation not only in terms of forgiveness of sins but in light of the total transformation of our lives. Dallas Willard presents a way of living that enables ordinary men and women to join with God and realize their highest aspirations of well-being and doing. The key to this self-transformation resides in the practice of the spiritual disciplines. Willard explains why the disciplines work and how their practice affirms human life to the fullest. (*www.amazon.com*)

Teaching the Word of Truth, by Donald Grey Barnhouse

This religious education material has stood the test of time because it is firmly anchored in the Word of God. Hundreds of dedicated Christian teachers have found in Barnhouse's lessons the guidance that has enabled them to expound biblical truth to young minds. The best book on biblical doctrine, it covers all of the main questions in simple user-friendly language and diagrams. (*www.amazon.com*)

Transitions: Making Sense of Life's Changes, by William Bridges

Strategies for coping with the difficult, painful and confusing times in your life. (*www.amazon.com*)

What Color Is Your Parachute? by Dick Bolles

For nearly thirty years, this book has been instrumental in helping people find a satisfying and fulfilling career. Answering the two questions, "What do you want to do?" and "Where do you want to do it?" gets you started in the right direction. This book is helpful for those just starting their career path as well as for those who are considering a career change. (*www.amazon.com*)

The Unfinished Presidency: Jimmy Carter's Journey Beyond the White House, by Douglas Brinkley

Most think Jimmy Carter is America's most effective ex-President. "The best of the new generation of American historians tell us in vigorous language the story of Carter's quite amazing range of activities at home and around the world."–Stephen Ambrose (*www.amazon.com*)

We Are the Beloved, by Ken Blanchard

This is a story about Ken's spiritual journey. In Ken's words, "This book is a meditation about God's unconditional love. I hope it helps you to think seriously about accepting this love, together with all the self-esteem, power, and freedom that brings. But if that does not happen, all is not lost. I still need the message myself." (*www.amazon.com*)

CONFERENCES/SEMINARS

Developing Your Game Plan Workshop

Provided by Halftime, the one-day workshop is designed to focus the participant on critical questions leading to developing a winning game plan for the Second Half of life. Explores gifts, talents, personal calling, and specific next steps. (*www.Halftime.org*)

Center for FaithWalk Leadership Conference

Founded by Ken Blanchard and Phil Hodges, the Center for FaithWalk Leadership hosts conferences across the country designed to stimulate personal spiritual growth. Participants are guided in exploring their response to Jesus' call to "Follow Me" and embrace the principles of servant leadership. 800–728–6000.

The Gathering Conference

Annual fall couples conference and regional conferences to help individuals, families and foundations giving significantly to Christian ministries expand their vision and be more effective. 903–509–9911.

Time Out Model

An annual event in Silicon Valley that brings leaders together to discover God's unique call on their lives and explore how to heed the call. It aims to provide a safe environment for people to: (1) reflect on their lives with their peers; (2) work towards balance among all their competing priorities; (3) invest their resources, talents, and gifts as God leads for maximum impact in the world. It's a good replicable model for other cities. For more information contact duane.moyer@Halftime.org.

Second Half Ministries Forums

An opportunity to experience, with your spouse, a meaningful midlife review. During three weekend forums, participants are guided through an enriching personal evaluation that becomes the foundation for a development plan for the Second Half of their lives. 719-594-2301. (*www.gospelcom.net/navs/secondhalf*)

The Trinity Forum

By invitation only. A leadership academy that helps leaders engage the key issues of their personal and public lives in the context of faith. Founded in 1991 as a nonprofit organization, it fosters strategic programs and publications that further its mission: to contribute to the transformation and renewal of society through the transformation and renewal of national leaders. (*www.ttf.org*)

AUDIOTAPES

Bob Buford's Favorite 12 Talks from The Foundation Conferences 1989–97

Contains 12 individual tapes by some of the world's top communicators: Millard Fuller, Ken Blanchard, Gordon MacDonald, Robert Wolgemuth, Bill Butterworth, Henri Nouwen, Bill Hybels, John Ortberg, Joe Stowell, and Larry Crabb. (*www.landesslezak.com/ccustore*)

Halftime: Men Facing Midlife

Bob Buford and Dennis Rainey. Family Life Today, a division of Campus Crusade for Christ. Tape #30413. 800-FLTODAY. (*www.familylife.com*)

Living a Legacy, Beyond Success to Significance

Bob Buford and Rick Warren. (*www.saddleback.com*)

Making Sense Out of Money: Leveraging Your Money for Eternity

Willow Creek Association, Resources. Bob Buford and Bill Hybels. (*www.willowcreek.org*)

Mars Hill Tapes

Since signing on in 1969, their approach to Christian programming has been a unique magazine format of traditional and inspirational music blended with conservative preaching/teaching and practical help programs. (*www.mhnetwork.org*)

Pastor to Pastor—Vol. 45-Spiritual Leadership in the 21ˢᵗ Century

Bob Buford with H. B. London. Focus on the Family. (*www.family.org*)

Strategies for Going from Success to Significance

Bob Buford. Young Presidents' Organization Vision & Values Seminar 1999. #2199–9203–03. (*www.penfield-prod.com/ypo/*)

Thinking Clearly About Spiritual Growth—Parable of The Sower, The Four Soils, Luke 8:4–15

Part 7 of a series on "Clear Thinking." From The Teaching Ministry of Rick Warren, senior pastor of Saddleback Church. Purpose Driven Resources, The Encouraging Word. 949–829–0300. (*www.pastors.com*)

William Wilberforce, A Man Who Changed His Times

"God Almighty has set before me two great objects: the suppression of the Slave Trade and the reformation of manners." William Wilberforce, a young parliamentarian, recorded this audacious ambition in his diary on October 28, 1787. Forty-six years later and three days before his death, slavery was abolished throughout the entire British Empire. Over the course of these years, he went from being one of the most vilified men in Europe to one of the most loved and revered in the world. This biographical account of Wilberforce's life and work was written by John Charles Pollock and is introduced by J. Douglas Holladay. Read by Ken Myers. A Trinity Forum Reading, produced on audiocassette by Mars Hill Audio. 800-331-6407. (*www.mhnetwork.org*)

LIFE COACHING

OnCourse™ International

Mentors, executives, and professionals who face challenging midlife issues. Jim Warner, founder and facilitator, has "walked in the shoes" of leaders so he can empathize with their issues, encouraging them to face change, and then help them chart course corrections for their personal life plan. Located in Boulder, Colorado. 303-449-7770.

CoachWorks® International.

Lee Smith, Jeannine Sandstrom, and George Ritcheske are a community of executive/leader coaches who deliver executive coaching services and products for business transition leadership success. Based in Dallas, Texas. 972-663-0301. (*www.coachworks.com*)

Family Wealth Counselors

By thinking beyond traditional estate planning, Family Wealth Counselors help families seize their remaining time, employ their unique talents, and mobilize their accumulated treasures to find fulfillment and significance as they discover and carry out their life purposes. (*www.fwc9dots.com/fwcoa.htm*)

The Hendricks Group

The Hendricks Group, based in Dallas, Texas, develops products and services that ensure the effective use of people in accomplishing meaningful and productive results. This involves individual assessment and coaching on the one hand and organizational assessment and alignment on the other. (*www.hendricksgroup.com*)

PathFinders

Char Lindner is the regional LifePlan facilitator for PathFinders, part of The Tom Paterson LifePlanners Association. Dedicated to helping believers discover their giftedness, Char's personal mission statement is "casual Christian to causal Christian." Based in Cincinnati, Ohio. 513–984–0588.

FINANCIAL

A Life Well Spent by Russ Crosson

When families weigh how their money can best be used, they need an eternal perspective. This book guides you toward that perspective by helping you move beyond a material view to a truly spiritual view of how money can do the most good. Published by Ronald Blue & Co., LLC.

Ron Blue & Co. – Professional, Bible-based financial counsel

Ronald Blue & Co. is a fee-only business providing personalized financial, estate, and investment counsel. It assists clients with managing their financial resources proactively and responsibly so they can experience peace of mind. It can help you address a wide array of Halftime issues, such as: How do I know I am making the right financial decisions? Can I retire? Am I using the best investment strategy? (*www.ronblue.com*)

Trinity Community Foundation

Created by Gordon Loux, Trinity Community Foundation assists families in designing giving plans that help the donors reach fulfilling and meaningful goals for their money. Based in Colorado Springs, CO. 719–473–1698.

Oxford Financial Advisors

Independent investment advisors to institutions, not for profit organizations, retirement plans, families, and individuals. (*www.oxfordgroupltd.com*)

SECOND HALF SERVICE/MINISTRY MODELS
The Barnabas Group

A partnership of Christian leaders who are committed to change their world and build God's kingdom through their irresistible lifestyles and influential works of service. Concepted by Bob Shank. For more information call 949–721–4191. *Prerequisite: The Master's Program.*

SHINE Model

Jim Beckett of Dallas, TX, hosts a weekly "quasi-brainstorming session" for marketplace peers and ministry leaders in the area. Low on formality but full of positive interaction, SHINE stands for Strategic consulting, Hospitality, Intercessory prayer, Networking, and Encouragement. It's a place where marketplace leaders can get in the game by sharing their time, talents, experience, and interest with ministry leaders. For more information, email Jim at jbeckett@beckett.com.

TCC Model

TCC groups meet monthly with a chairman/facilitator. In the morning they are challenged and encouraged by an outside trainer on a variety of topics vital to their transition or service/ministries. In the afternoon group members become a resource to one another, iron sharpening iron, as TCC members boldly share their challenges, fears, and opportunities. Then, in the course of each month, the chairman spends at least two hours with each TCC member in private coaching sessions. Fred Chaney, who developed this model, is available to come to your city and help you establish a TCC group for your area. 940–440–9438.

Discover God's Special Calling
for the Second Half of Life

HALFTIME

*Changing Your Game Plan
from Success to Significance*

Bob Buford

0-310-23275-9

Five interactive sessions based on
the best-selling book by Bob Buford

Interactive Format–Specially Designed
for Groups of Any Size

Bob Buford's best-selling book, *Halftime,* struck a universal chord with men and women from many walks of life and socioeconomic backgrounds. As they approach the midpoint of life, many find themselves asking, *What do I do now that I've grown up? Is this all there is to life? What can I do to find more meaning and significance? Why am I so restless? Is there life after success?*

A businessman, seminar leader, and friend, Bob Buford has guided thousands of people toward lives of personal significance. This video series makes the halftime process available to thousands more. The series features insightful video presentations of men and men involved in the *Halftime* journey. It will help participants tap into their unique set of gifts and abilities, opportunities and relationships, inner desires and dreams, and God-given callings. It will help them discover the key to a significant life and will help them chart a course that will make the second half of their lives the best half.

Includes:

- Five video presentations on one 80-minute VHS video.
- Five group sessions (each approximately 55 minutes long, including video and discussion).
- Easy-to-use, comprehensive Leader's Guide (extra guides sold separately) featuring discussion topics, practical application sections, etc. Leaders can amplify points with their own illustrations and/or materials.
- Easy-to-follow Participant's Guide (extra guides sold separately) with supplemental resource material for ongoing personal growth.
- Paperback *Halftime* book by Bob Buford.

"I have discovered that life change occurs locally, over time, with others...basically in community. Halftime ZondervanGroupware™ is designed with this in mind and is an excellent step for those who desire to embrace God's calling and move from success to significance."
Ken Blanchard, Author, *One Minute Manager*

For more information about the movement known as
Halftime, visit www.Halftime.org

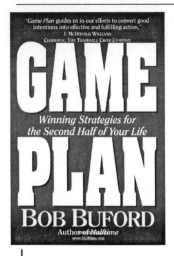

We want to hear from you. Please send your comments about this book to us in care of the address below. Thank you.

GRAND RAPIDS, MICHIGAN 49530 USA

WWW.ZONDERVAN.COM